Abingdon's

Where the Bible Comes to Life

In the Garden

Preschool

Also available from Abingdon Press:

Abingdon's BibleZone® LIVE
Younger Elementary
FUNspirational® Kit

Abingdon's BibleZone® LIVE
Older Elementary
FUNspirational® Kit

Writer: Elizabeth Parr
Editor: Susan Groseclose
Production Editor: Karen Williams
Managing Editor: LeeDell Stickler
Production and Design Manager:
R.E. Osborne
Designer: Paige Easter
Front Cover Photo: Ron Benedict
Illustrator: Robert S. Jones

Abingdon's Bible Zone Preschool LIVE

Where the Bible Comes to Life

IN THE GARDEN

Abingdon Press
Nashville

Abingdon's
BibleZone® LIVE
Where the Bible Comes to Life
IN THE GARDEN
Preschool

Copyright © 2003 Abingdon Press

All rights reserved.

No part of this work, EXCEPT PATTERNS AND PAGES COVERED BY THE NOTICE BELOW, may be reproduced or transmitted in any form or by any means, electronic or mechanical, including photocopying and recording, or by any information storage or retrieval system, except as may be expressly permitted by the 1976 Copyright Act or by permission in writing from the publisher. Requests for permission should be submitted in writing to: Abingdon Press, 201 Eighth Avenue South, Nashville, TN 37203, faxed to (615) 749-6128, or submitted via email to *permission@abingdonpress.com*.

• NOTICE •
ONLY PATTERNS / PAGES that are marked **Reproducible**
may be duplicated for use in the local church or church school.
The following copyright notice is included on these pages and must appear on the reproduction:

Permission granted to photocopy for local church use. © 2003 Abingdon Press.

Unless otherwise noted, Scripture quotations are from the Contemporary English Version, © 1991, 1992, 1995 by the American Bible Society. Used by permission.

ISBN 0-687-09254-X

Art by Robert S. Jones; art on p. 15 © 1999 Abingdon Press.

03 04 05 06 07 08 09 11 12 13—10 9 8 7 6 5 4 3 2 1

MANUFACTURED IN THE UNITED STATES OF AMERICA

Table of Contents
In the Garden

Bible Units in the Zone 6
About BibleZone® 7
Welcome to the BibleZone® 8
Preschool 9
Shout Hosanna! 10
Remember Me 22
Watch With Me 34
I Don't Know Him 46
The Garden Tomb 58
Good News in the Garden 70
No Garden At All 82
Let There Be Light 94
Filling the Garden 106
Tending the Garden 118
God's First Garden (Adam and Eve) 130
The Naming 142
A Time for All Things 154
GameZone 166
SnackZone 167
ArtZone 168
Reproducible 7C 169
Nametags 170
All About You 171
Happy Birthday Note 172
Reproducible 9C 173
BZ Bee 174
Comments From Users 175

Bible Units in the Zone

1. Lent and Easter

Bible Story	Bible Verse
Shout Hosanna!	Mark 11:1-11; Luke 19:28-38
Remember Me	Matthew 26:17-30; Luke 22:7-23
Watch With Me	Matthew 26:36-46; Mark 14:32-42
I Don't Know Him	Luke 22:54-62; John 18:15-18, 25-27
The Garden Tomb	Luke 23:44-56; John 19:38-42
Good News in the Garden	Luke 24:1-12

2. Creation

Bible Story	Bible Verse
No Garden At All	Genesis 1:1-13
Let There Be Light	Genesis 1:14-19
Filling the Garden	Genesis 1:9-13, 20-25
Tending the Garden	Genesis 1:26-31
God's First Garden (Adam and Eve)	Genesis 2:4-17; 3:1-13, 20-24
The Naming	Genesis 2:18-24
A Time for All Things	Ecclesiastes 3:1-15

About BibleZone LIVE

ZoneZillies:

ZoneZillies® are game and storytelling props found in the BibleZone® FUNspirational® Kit. Some ZoneZillies® are consumable and will need to be replaced. These are added for the teacher's convenience.

- cross antenna topper
- inflatable elephant and rings
- butterfly fans
- CD
- butterfly stamps
- inflatable ball
- jumbo monkey
- animal stickers
- zoo animal porcupine balls
- zoo animal finger puppets
- plastic baskets
- plastic Easter eggs

Supplies:

- Bible
- paper punch & scissors
- tempera paint, stained glass paint, paintbrushes, paint cups, paint roller, paint shirts
- glue
- ribbons, cloth, yarn, fabric scraps
- markers & crayons
- paper plates and cups, paper towels, plastic spoons
- a variety of tape
- streamers or ribbons
- stapler
- envelopes
- spools
- coat hangers with cardboard on them
- Styrofoam meat trays
- drop cloth
- heart stickers, star stickers, fish stickers
- contact paper or laminating film
- flour, iodized salt, white vinegar, kernels of popcorn, ice
- puzzle pieces painted red
- piece of dry wall or a bed sheet, plastic sheeting, fiberfill, foam pieces
- brown grocery bags & plastic bag
- newspapers
- cupcake liners
- large craft sticks
- clear sealing spray
- fishing line
- posterboard, cardboard, cardboard tubes, shoe boxes, cardboard paper roll
- feathers
- a variety of paper
- instant camera with film
- brads, safety pins, buttons, Velcro
- pieces of foil, glitter, confetti
- coffee filters
- chenille stems
- wooden clothespins, wiggly eyes
- potting soil and/or sod, silk flowers, rocks, leaves, sand clay, potting soil
- scarves, clothing for different kinds of weather
- bowls, shallow pans, flat pan or dish, cookie sheet, rolling pin, whisk or hand eggbeater, spoon
- cotton swabs
- bed sheet or bulletin board paper
- sponges
- old socks or rubber band
- toothpicks
- aluminum foil, plastic wrap, sandwich bags
- fake fur
- clothesbasket, small dish tub, squirt bottle, mild detergent flakes
- mirrors
- inkpad
- salt clay
- bubble alphabet letters
- toothbrushes

Welcome to BibleZone LIVE

Where the Bible Comes to Life

Have fun learning about favorite Bible stories from the Old and New Testaments. Each lesson in this teacher guide is filled with games and activities that will make learning FUNspirational® for you and your students. With just a few added supplies, everything you need to teach is included in the Abingdon's BibleZone® Live FUNspirational® Kit.

Each lesson has a ZoneIn® box:

 **We thank God for the seasons.**

that is repeated over and over again throughout the lesson.
The ZoneIn® states the Bible message in words your students will connect to their lives.

Use the following tips to help make your trip into BibleZone® Live a FUNspirational® success!

- Read through each lesson. Read the Bible passages.
- Memorize the Bible verse and the ZoneIn® statement.
- Choose the activities that fit your unique group of students and your time limitations.
- Read the BibleZone® story.
- Gather the ZoneZillies® you will use for the lesson.
- Gather supplies you will use for the lesson.
- Learn the music for the lesson from the BibleZone® FUNspirational® CD.
- Arrange your room space so there is plenty of room for the students to move and sit on the floor.
- Photocopy the Reproducible pages for the lesson.
- Photocopy the HomeZone® page for students.

Preschool

Each child in your class is a one-of-a-kind child of God. Each child has his or her own name, background, family situation, and set of experiences. It is important to remember and celebrate each child's uniqueness. Yet all of these one-of-a-kind children of God have some common needs.
- All children need love.
- All children need a sense of self-worth.
- All children need to feel a sense of accomplishment.
- All children need to have a safe place to be and to express their feelings.
- All children need to be surrounded by adults who love them.
- All children need to experience the love of God.

Preschoolers (children ages 3–5 years old) also have some common characteristics.

Their Bodies
- They do not sit still for very long.
- They have lots of energy.
- They enjoy moving (running, galloping, dancing, jumping, hopping).
- They are developing fine motor skills (learning to cut with scissors, learning to handle a ball, learning to tie their shoes).
- They enjoy using their senses (tasting, touching, smelling, hearing, seeing).

Their Minds
- They are learning more and more words.
- They enjoy music.
- They are learning to express their feelings.
- They like to laugh and can be silly.
- They enjoy nonsense words.
- They are learning to identify colors, sizes, and shapes.
- They have an unclear understanding of time.
- They have a wonderful imagination.

Their Relationships
- They are beginning to interact with others as they play together.
- They are beginning to understand that other people have feelings.
- They are learning to wait for their turn.
- They can have a hard time leaving parents, especially mother.
- They want to help.
- They love to feel important.

Their Hearts
- They need to handle the Bible and see others handle it.
- They need caring adults who model Christian attitudes and behaviors.
- They need to sing, move to, and say Bible verses.
- They need to hear clear, simple stories from the Bible.
- They can express simple prayers.
- They can experience wonder and awe at God's world.
- They can share food and money and make things for others.
- They can experience belonging at church.

1 Bible ZONE LIVE

Shout Hosanna!

Enter the Zone

Bible Verse
Blessed is the king who comes in the name of the Lord!

(Luke 19:38)

Bible Story
Mark 11:1-11; Luke 19:28-38

The Scripture today tells the story of Jesus' entry into Jerusalem. Jesus sends two of his disciples into the village instructing them to bring him a young donkey on which he would ride. The only directions that we read in the Scripture are that the disciples will find a donkey as they enter the village. The directions are not very specific; yet, the disciples are able to find the donkey. If anyone notices that the disciples are taking the young donkey, Jesus instructs them to say, "The Lord needs it" (Luke 19:31). This answer is sufficient for the people who observe the disciples taking the young donkey. There is no concern expressed by the owners that these two men are walking off with their possession.

The scene in which Jesus enters Jerusalem was a happy and triumphant scene. The people gathered on the sides of the road to see Jesus ride by on the young donkey. They spread their cloaks on the ground and waved branches that they had cut from the field in order to show respect and thanksgiving for Jesus.

This was a custom usually reserved for the anointing of kings. It was recognition of Jesus as the Messiah, the king who would deliver his people.

The Gospel of Mark describes the people cutting branches from the field. The description of the branches as palm branches only appears in the Gospel of John. The Gospel of Luke refers only to the people placing clothes on the road. Because we celebrate this entry into Jerusalem on Palm Sunday, we will have palm branches to wave.

Hosanna is the word the people chanted as Jesus rode by. This literally means "save us now." This was the plea of the people for deliverance. As we talk with young children, we will focus on Hosanna as praise for Jesus. Young children will not understand the significance of Jesus' entry into Jerusalem. They can, however, identify with the celebration and the excitement the people felt when they saw Jesus.

We praise God for Jesus.

Scope the Zone

ZONE	TIME	SUPPLIES	ZILLIES
Zoom Into the Zone			
Happy Hosanna Hats	8 minutes	heavy paper bowls, paper punch, scissors, yarn, tempera paint, glue, ribbon, wrapping paper, art tissue, feathers	none
Traveling on the Road	7 minutes	Reproducible 1A, cloth, yarn, markers or crayons, glue	none
BibleZone®			
Hosanna Hoops	5 minutes	small paper plates, tape, scissors, green crepe paper, streamers, stapler	none
Hosanna Hop	2 minutes	none	none
Shout Hosanna!	5 minutes	hosanna hoops	none
Bible Verse Buzz	5 minutes	Bible, BZ Bee	none
Praisin' and Singin'	5 minutes	CD player	CD
Saying and Seeing	5 minutes	Reproducible 1B, scissors, markers, envelopes	none
LifeZone			
Hosanna Hoopla	3 minutes	Hosanna hats and hoops, CD player	CD
Remember With Ellie	3 minutes	none	inflatable elephant and rings
Thank You Banner	10 minutes	tempera paint, spools, coat hangers, colored duct tape, meat trays, drop cloth, butcher paper, palm branches	none
Butterfly Prayers	2 minutes	none	butterfly fans

Zillies® are found in the **BibleZone® LIVE FUNspirational® Kit.**

Preschool: Lesson 1

Zoom Into the Zone

Choose one or more activities to catch your children's interest.

Supplies:
small, heavy paper bowls, 1 per child
paper punch
scissors
yarn
tempera paint
glue
ribbon, wrapping paper, tissue paper
feathers

Zillies®:
none

Happy Hosanna Hats

Give each child a bowl. Punch a hole in each side of the bowl. Using the feathers, have the children paint their hats. While the paint is still wet, let them decorate the hat with the ribbon, wrapping paper, tissue paper, and so forth. You may need to add extra glue depending on the amount of paint the child uses. Insert a 12-inch length of yarn into the punched hole on each side of the hat. Put them aside to dry so they can be used later in the lesson.

Say: When Jesus rode the donkey into Jerusalem, all of the people were so happy. They hurried to the side of the road to see Jesus. We're making our Happy Hosanna Hats to remind us of that happy day. We are happy that God sent Jesus to us.

We praise God for Jesus.

Supplies:
Reproducible 1A
small pieces of cloth
small pieces of brown or gray yarn
markers or crayons
glue

Zillies®:
none

Traveling on the Road

Give each child a copy of the picture of Jesus riding on the young donkey into Jerusalem **(Reproducible 1A)**.

Say: When Jesus rode the donkey into Jerusalem, the people hurried out to see him. They were so excited that they laid their clothes down by the road to honor Jesus. We're going to make a picture to remind us of this special day.

Have the children color their picture. Add yarn for the donkey's mane and tail. Glue pieces of cloth to the road.

BibleZone® LIVE

Bible

Choose one or more activities to immerse your children in the Bible story.

Hosanna Hoops

Before class, cut the center out of the paper plates. Give each child two paper plate rings. Ask the children to tape the crepe paper streamers on one side of one of the rings. Place the other ring on top and let the child help you staple the two together.

Say: When the people saw Jesus coming down the road riding on a donkey, they waved branches they had cut from the fields. We are going to use our Hosanna Hoops to praise Jesus. These will be our branches.

Use hoops in the "Hosanna Hop" and during story time.

Hosanna Hop

Use the "Hosanna Hop" to lead your children to the story area.

Hosanna, Hosanna, this is what we say
(Wave hoops overhead in an arc.)
Hosanna, Hosanna, we can shout hooray.
(Jump up in the air, shouting hooray.)
We love to hear the stories that tell us of the way
(Cup hand to ear.)
Jesus taught us how to live and love God everyday.
(Point up and hug self.)
Hosanna, Hosanna, let's stomp on down the road.
(Stomp along.)
Hosanna, Hosanna, let's ride like Jesus rode.
(Pretend to ride donkey.)
Hosanna, Hosanna, let's hop on down the road.
(Hop along.)
Hosanna, Hosanna, let's ride like Jesus rode.
(Pretend to ride donkey.)
Hosanna, Hosanna, this is what we say
(Wave hoops over head in an arc.)
Hosanna, Hosanna, we can shout hooray.
(Jump up in the air, shouting hooray.)

Supplies:
small paper plates,
   2 per child
tape
scissors
green crepe paper
   streamers cut in
   12-inch lengths
stapler

Zillies®:
none

Supplies:
none

Zillies®:
none

PRESCHOOL: LESSON 1

Bible Story

Shout Hosanna!

by Beth Parr

Have the children sit in a circle. Ask the children to help to tell the story by doing the motions and waving their hosanna hoops.

Walking, walking, walking.
(Pretend to walk in place.)
Jesus and his disciples had been traveling for a long time. They were headed to Jerusalem. One day Jesus sent two of his disciples ahead to the next town. He told them they would find a young donkey there.
"Bring the donkey back to me. Tell the owners it will be returned."

Searching, searching, searching.
(Shade eyes with hand, looking back and forth.)
The disciples found the donkey. They told the owners that Jesus needed it and that it would be returned.
The disciples brought the donkey back to Jesus.

Riding, riding, riding.
(Pretend to ride the donkey.)
Jesus climbed on the back of the donkey. He was riding the donkey into Jerusalem.

Cheering, cheering, cheering.
(Wave hands, cheer.)
As Jesus got closer to Jerusalem, he could hear the people cheering. There were lots and lots of people standing by the road. Some of them were waving palm branches. Some had put their coats on the road. They were so excited that Jesus was coming. They were so happy.

Hosanna, Hosanna, Hosanna.
(Wave hosanna hoops overhead.)
The people were saying hosanna. They were so happy that Jesus was coming. They were glad that Jesus was God's Son.

Hosanna, Hosanna, Hosanna.
(Wave hosanna hoops overhead.)
The people said, "Blessed is the king who comes in the name of the Lord." They were glad that God had sent Jesus to help them live God's way.

Hosanna, Hosanna, Hosanna.
(Wave hosanna hoops overhead.)

Save the hosanna hoops to use later in this lesson and with the next lessons in this unit.

In With BZ Bee

Bible Verse Buzz

Choose a child to hold the Bible open to Luke 19:38.

Say: God sent Jesus to teach people about God. Our Bible story today tells us about how happy the people were to see Jesus when he rode the donkey into Jerusalem.

Say the Bible verse, "Blessed is the king who comes in the name of the Lord!" (Luke 19:38), for the children.

Have the children say the Bible verse after you.

Turn your back to the children or hide your hands underneath a table as you place the BZ Bee puppet (see page 174) on your hand. Turn around or bring the puppet out where the children can see it.

Pretend to make the puppet talk. Change your voice for the puppet:

Bzzz, Bzzz, Bzzz. Hi, everybody! I'm BZ Bee.

Bzzz, Bzzz, Bzzz. I like to taste ears. Do you have ears? Yum, yum, yum. Let me taste.

Go to each child. Encourage, but do not force each child to turn his or her ear toward BZ. Have BZ pretend to taste each child's ears. Have BZ say things like:

**Mmmm. Mmmm. You taste like honey.
Bzzz. Bzzz. You taste like apples.
Yumm. Yumm. You taste like peaches.**

After BZ has tasted each child's ears, **say: Bzzz. Bzzz. Bzzz. I like to taste your ears. They're yummy.** *(Rub BZ's stomach)*

Bzzz. Bzzz. Bzzz. I like something else even more than ears. I like the Bible.

Bzzz. Bzzz. Bzzz. You heard a Bible story today. Who was the man in the Bible story? *(Jesus)* **What did Jesus do?** *(rode a donkey into Jerusalem)* **What did the people do and say when they saw Jesus?** *(They waved palm branches, put their coats in the road, and said Hosanna.)*

Bzzz. Bzzz. Bzzz. God sent Jesus to teach us more about God. We are happy that Jesus loves us.

We praise God for Jesus.

Bzzz. Bzzz. Bzzz. Let's say the Bible verse together: "Blessed is the king who comes in the name of the Lord!" (Luke 19:38)

Have the children repeat the Bible verse with BZ Bee.

Have BZ Bee say good-bye to the children. Put the puppet away.

PRESCHOOL: LESSON 1

Bible

Choose one or more activities to immerse your children in the Bible story.

Supplies:
CD player

Zillies®:
CD

Praisin' and Singin'

Say: The people on the road were so excited about seeing Jesus. They praised God for Jesus. We can praise God as we sing.

Sing the song, "Praisin'," from the **CD (Track 13)**. Do the motions that go along with the song.

Praisin'

Cap, clap! *(Clap hands.)*
Ain't it great to be praisin'
Clap, clap! *(Clap hands.)*
Ain't it great to be praisin',
Praisin' the Lord with all our friends.
Clap, clap! *(Clap hands.)*
Ain't it great to be praisin'.

Stomp, stomp! *(Stomp feet.)*
Ain't it great to be praisin'
Stomp, stomp! *(Stomp feet.)*
Ain't it great to be praisin',
Praisin' the Lord with all our friends.
Stomp, stomp! *(Stomp feet.)*
Ain't it great to be praisin'.

Shake, shake! *(Shake hands with a friend.)*
Ain't it great to be praisin'
Shake, shake! *(Shake hands with a friend.)*
Ain't it great to be praisin',
Praisin' the Lord with all our friends.
Shake, shake! *(Shake hands with a friend.)*
Ain't it great to be praisin'.

Bump, bump! *(Bump hips with a friend.)*
Ain't it great to be praisin'
Bump, bump! *(Bump hips with a friend.)*
Ain't it great to be praisin',
Praisin' the Lord with all our friends.
Bump, bump! *(Bump hips with a friend.)*
Ain't it great to be praisin'.

WORDS: Daphna Flegal
Words © 2001 Abingdon Press

Supplies:
Reproducible 1B,
   1 per child
scissors
crayons and markers
envelopes or
   sandwich bags

Zillies®:
none

Saying and Seeing

Give each child a copy of the sequence cards **(Reproducible 1B)**. Have them color the pictures on the sequence cards. Help them to cut the cards apart. Mix the cards up.

Say: Can you help me tell the story with these cards? What happened first in our story? *(Jesus and the disciples were walking along.)* **And then?** *(Jesus sent two disciples to get the donkey.)* **And then?** *(The men found the donkey and brought it back to Jesus.)* **And then?** *(The disciples helped Jesus get on the donkey.)* **And then?** *(Jesus rode the donkey into Jerusalem.)* **And then?** *(The people waved palm branches and shouted hosanna.)*

Let the children scramble the cards again and try to put them in order on their own. Place the cards into envelopes or sandwich bags for the children to take home.

Say: You can tell your family the story today with your cards. We are so happy that Jesus loves us.

BibleZone® LIVE

Life Zone

Choose one or more activities to bring the Bible to life.

Hosanna Hoopla

Have the children put on their hats and get their hoops. Form a line. Locate "Sanna, Sannanina" on the **CD (Track 1)**.

Say: Our Bible story taught us that people were so excited to see Jesus. They were glad that God sent Jesus to them. We can praise God for Jesus too. We're going to march around the room as we listen to a special praise song from Africa. We'll wave our Hosanna hoops and praise God for Jesus.

Enjoy moving around the room and waving the streamers. End by saying, "Hosanna!"

Supplies:
hosanna hats and hoops made earlier
CD player

Zillies®:
CD

Remembering With Ellie the Elephant

Have the children sit in a circle. Practice saying the Bible verse (Luke 19:38) with the children by saying the first part of the verse, "Blessed is the king" and help them to respond, "who comes in the name of the Lord." Do this several times. Place Ellie the Elephant in the middle of the circle.

Say: We're going to play a little game with our friend, Ellie the Elephant. I'll pick one of you to take one of these rings and put it on Ellie's nose. I'm going to say the first part of our Bible verse. Then we'll all say the rest of the verse.

Play this until every child who wants a turn has had a chance.

Supplies:
none

Zillies®:
inflatable elephant and rings

 **We praise God for Jesus.**

PRESCHOOL: LESSON 1

Life

Choose one or more activities to bring the Bible to life.

Supplies:
tempera paint
spools (thread, ribbon, and so forth)
coat hangers with cardboard on them
colored duct tape
meat trays (clean with bleach solution)
drop cloth
butcher paper
palm branches

Zillies®:
none

Thank You Banner

Before class, follow these directions to make Racy Rollers. Take the cardboard tubes off the hangers. Cut the wires so that each is about five inches long. Bend the ends of the wire at a 90-degree angle. Put the ends into an empty thread or ribbon spool. Make sure it rolls easily. Wrap colored duct tape around the handle for safety.

Say: We want to thank God for Jesus. We are happy and want to praise Jesus just like the people in our story.

Cover the table with a drop cloth or newspaper. Have the children spread the palm branches out all over the table. On the butcher paper, write "Thank God for Jesus" and "Hosanna." Place the butcher paper over the table and tape the ends down.

Pour small amounts of paint in the meat trays. Roll the Racy Roller in the paint and then roll it all over the paper. In the places where the palm branches are, they will see the outline of the palm branch.

After the banner dries, hang it outside the door of your classroom.

Supplies:
none

Zillies®:
butterfly fans

Butterfly Prayers

Have the children sit down in the worship area. Give each child a fan. If you have a large group, you can do this more than once and let them share the fans.

Say: Today we learned about how happy the people were to see Jesus. They praised God for Jesus. We can praise God for Jesus too.

Ask the children to wave their fans in front of them the first three lines of the poem. On the last line, the children will raise their fan and wave it over their head.

> Waving fans can be such fun
> Cool air blows on everyone.
> Wave your fans and let's shout hooray
> We praise God for Jesus today.

Pray: Dear God, Thank you for loving us. Thank you for Jesus, your special Son. Amen.

Photocopy the HomeZone newsletter to send home to the parents.

BibleZone® LIVE

Home Zone For Parents

Bible Verse
Blessed is the king who comes in the name of the Lord!
Luke 19:38

Bible Story
Mark 11:1-11; Luke 19:28-38

Today we shared the story of Jesus riding the donkey into Jerusalem. The people were so happy to see Jesus. They knew that God had sent Jesus to help them live in God's way. With young children, we emphasize the excitement and joy of the people as they greeted Jesus. It is difficult for them to understand all that Jesus represented to the people in Jerusalem.

We learned the word *hosanna*. While this actually means "please save us," we have compared it to the word *hooray*. This helps the children to know how much the people were looking forward to Jesus coming into their town.

Hosanna Handprint Cookies

You will need: your favorite sugar cookie recipe or commercially made cookie dough, plastic knife, sprinkles, egg yolk, and food coloring.

On a floured surface, roll out the cookie dough until it is about one half inch thick. Have your child lay their hand on top of the dough. Use a plastic knife to carefully cut out their hand shape. Let them decorate the cookies with sprinkles. One option is to decorate the cookies with egg paint. Mix an egg yolk with one-fourth teaspoon of water. Divide it into smaller containers. Add food coloring to the egg yolk. Let your child "paint" the cookie before baking. If the paint gets thick, add a little more water. Share these at home or with family and friends.

We praise God for Jesus.

PRESCHOOL: LESSON 1   Permission granted to photocopy for local church use. © 2003 Abingdon Press.

Reproducible 1A

Preschool: Lesson 1 — Reproducible 1B

Permission granted to photocopy for local church use. © 2003 Abingdon Press.

Remember Me

Enter the Zone

Bible Verse
Remember me.
(I Corinthians 11:24)

Bible Story
Matthew 26:17-30; Luke 22:7-23

The Scripture today tells the story of Jesus celebrating a last Passover meal with his disciples. We refer to this event as The Last Supper. Passover was a special Jewish festival time in which the people of Israel remembered that God had rescued them from slavery in Egypt. The special foods that the people ate reminded them of specific parts of their rescue story. The Feast of the Unleavened Bread began the day after Passover. This festival reminded the Jewish people of how quickly they had to leave Egypt. They didn't even have time for their bread to rise. It was likewise a time to give thanks for the grain harvest. These celebrations were very holy times for the Jewish people. In our story today, Jesus and his disciples are sharing the Passover or Passover eve meal together.

It is also at this time that Jesus tells the disciples to eat the bread and drink the wine to remember him. These passages are some of the passages that are reflected in our celebration of the Lord's Supper.

We celebrate communion to remember Jesus and his sacrifice for us. It is a time to renew our commitment to live, as God wants us to live.

In Bible times, as today, having a meal together was much more than just eating. It was sharing God's goodness. It was fellowship with other members of the family of God. Young children enjoy the times when their families gather for special meals, such as Thanksgiving or Christmas or Easter.

They will not understand the symbolism of the bread and wine, even if they have participated in communion with their family. Our emphasis is on this being a special meal that Jesus and his disciples had, just as we have special times with our families. It is also a special time in our church when we remember Jesus and we know that Jesus loves us.

We remember that Jesus loves us.

Scope the Zone

ZONE	TIME	SUPPLIES	ZILLIES®
Zoom Into the Zone			
Looking and Remembering	10 minutes	Reproducible 2A, crayons or markers	none
Heart-y Placemats	10 minutes	Reproducible 2B, heart stickers, markers or crayons, clear contact paper or laminating film	none
BibleZone®			
Remember the Meal	5 minutes	4 cups flour, 1 cup iodized salt, 1 1 cups warm water, bowl	none
Sing and Sign	5 minutes	CD player	CD
Remember Me	5 minutes	none	none
Bible Verse Buzz	2 minutes	Bible, BZ Bee	none
Praisin' and Singin'	5 minutes	CD player	CD
Remembering Game	5 minutes	5 items (Bible, paintbrush, CD, and so forth), cloth	none
LifeZone			
Jesus Loves Me Pins	5 minutes	hearts cut out of posterboard, puzzle pieces painted red, glue, safety pins or tape, smaller heart that says "Jesus Loves Me"	none
Remember With Ellie	5 minutes	CD Player	CD, inflatable elephant and rings
Butterfly Prayers	3 minutes	none	butterfly fans

Zillies® are found in the **BibleZone® LIVE FUNspirational® Kit.**

PRESCHOOL: LESSON 2

Zoom Into the Zone

Choose one or more activities to capture the attention of your children.

Supplies:
Reproducible 2A
crayons or markers

Zillies®:
none

Looking and Remembering

Give each child a picture of Jesus and his disciples **(Reproducible 2A)**. There are two different pictures of Jesus and his disciples eating at the table. Ask the children to look at the picture on the top of the page. Now look at the picture on the bottom of the page.

Say: What do you see that is different? *(Allow time for the children to share their answers.)*

They then can color the pictures with crayons or markers.

Say: Jesus had a special meal with his friends. He loved his friends. He loves you and me. We can always remember that Jesus loves us.

We remember that Jesus loves us.

Supplies:
Reproducible 2B
heart stickers
markers or crayons
contact paper or
laminating film

Zillies®:
none

Heart-y Placemats

Give each child a copy of the placemat **(Reproducible 2B)** with "Jesus loves me" on it.

Have the children color their placemats and decorate them with stickers.

Say: When Jesus had the special meal with his disciples, he wanted them to remember that he loved them. We remember he loves us too. When you use your placemat, you can remember that Jesus loves you. Cover the placemat with contact paper or laminating film to protect it from spills.

We remember that Jesus loves us.

BibleZone® LIVE

Bible

Choose one or more activities to immerse your children in the Bible story.

Remember the Meal

Combine all the ingredients in a bowl. Allow the children to help mix the dough together. Mix together well. Knead the dough for about 10 minutes.

Say: In our story today, Jesus has a special meal with his friends. He tells his friends that they should remember him when they eat bread and drink juice together. Let's make a cup and plate like Jesus might have used.

Give each child a ball of dough. Show them how to push their fingers into the ball to make a cup. Give them another ball of dough to flatten into a plate.

The dishes can be baked at 300 degrees until they are hard or can air dry in a few days.

Supplies:
4 cups flour
1 cup iodized salt
1 ¾ cups warm water
bowl

Zillies®:
none

Sing and Sign

Sing together the song, "Bread and Juice," to the tune of "Hot Cross Buns" **(CD Track 14)**.

Bread and juice
Bread and juice
Jesus shared a special meal of
Bread and juice.

Bread and juice
Bread and juice
We remember Jesus with our
Bread and juice.

Based on Mark 14:12-16; 22-25
WORDS: Daphna Flegal
Words © 2001 Abingdon Press

Supplies:
CD player

Zillies®:
CD

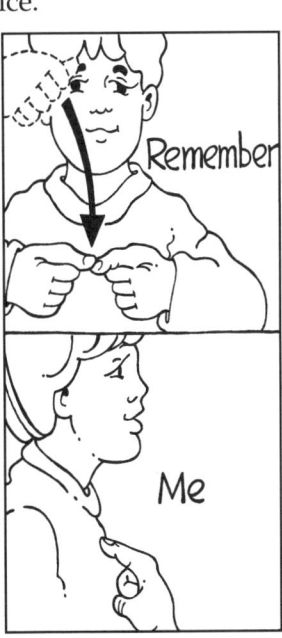

Teach the children the Bible verse "Remember me" (I Corinthians 11:24) in American Sign Language.
To sign the word *remember* – Curl both hands into fist with the thumbs out. Touch the right thumb to your forehead. Bring your right fist down alongside of your face and then place your right thumb on top of your left thumb.
To sign the word *me* – Point the index finger of your right hand toward your chest.

PRESCHOOL: LESSON 2

Bible Zone Story

Remember Me

by Beth Parr

Use the "Hosanna Hop" to lead your children to the story area. (See Lesson 1, page 13.) Have the children sit in a circle. Ask the children to help tell the story by signing, "Remember Me" when it appears in the story. Instructions to sign "remember me" appear on page 28 and below.

Remember me, remember me.
Were words that Jesus said.
Remember me, remember me.
Come, share the juice and bread.

Passover was a special time of celebration and remembering. Jesus and his disciples were getting ready to celebrate Passover. Jesus sent two of his friends, Peter and John, to get things ready for everyone.

Remember me, remember me.
Were words that Jesus said.
Remember me, remember me.
Come, share the juice and bread.

As Jesus and his friends ate together, Jesus held up a cup of grape juice. He thanked God for the juice. He told his disciples to drink juice together and to remember him.

Remember me, remember me.
Were words that Jesus said.
Remember me, remember me.
Come, share the juice and bread.

Jesus also lifted up the bread. He thanked God for the bread. He told his disciples to eat the bread together and to remember him.

Remember me, remember me.
Were words that Jesus said.
Remember me, remember me.
Come, share the juice and bread.

After they had finished eating, Jesus and his friends sang a song together. The disciples knew that Jesus loved them. They would always remember Jesus and his love.

Remember me, remember me.
Were words that Jesus said.
Remember me, remember me.
Come, share the juice and bread.

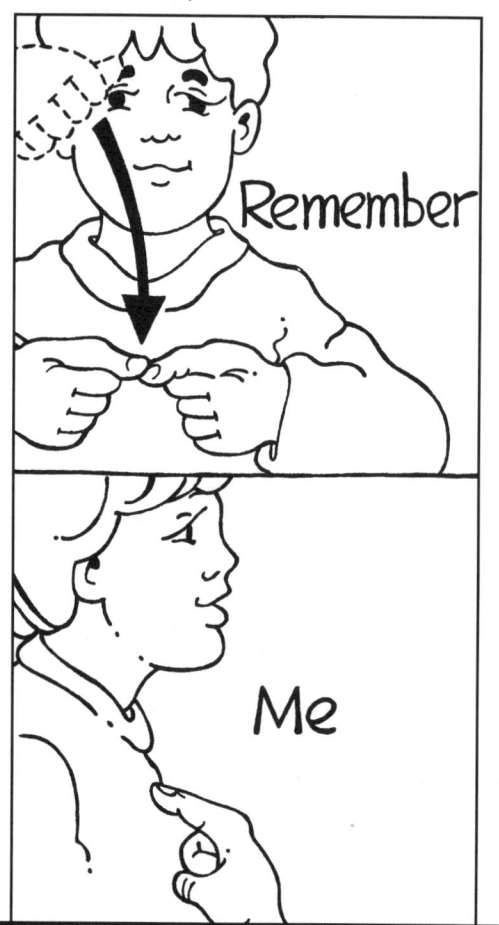

BibleZone® LIVE

In With BZ Bee

Bible Verse Buzz

Choose a child to hold the Bible open to I Corinthians 11:24.

Say: Jesus wanted his disciples to remember that he loved them. They had a special meal together. The disciples knew that Jesus loved them.

Say the Bible verse, "Remember me" (I Corinthians 11:24), for the children. Have the children say the Bible verse after you.

Turn your back to the children or hide your hands underneath a table as you place the BZ Bee puppet (see page 174) on your hand. Turn around or bring the puppet out where the children can see it.

Pretend to make the puppet talk. Change your voice for the puppet:

Bzzz, Bzzz, Bzzz. Hi, everybody! I'm BZ Bee.

Bzzz, Bzzz, Bzzz. I like to taste ears. Do you have ears? Yum, yum, yum. Let me taste.

Go to each child. Encourage, but do not force each child to turn his or her ear toward BZ. Have BZ pretend to taste each child's ears. Have BZ say things like:

**Mmmm. Mmmm. You taste like honey.
Bzzz. Bzzz. You taste like apples.
Yumm. Yumm. You taste like peaches.**

After BZ has tasted each child's ears, **say: Bzzz. Bzzz. Bzzz. I like to taste your ears. They're yummy.** (Rub BZ's stomach.)

Bzzz. Bzzz. Bzzz. I like something else even more than ears. I like the Bible. Bzzz. Bzzz. Bzzz. You heard a Bible story today. What did Jesus and his disciples do together? (They had a special meal.) **What did Jesus want his disciples to always do?** (remember him) **What special food did they share together?** (bread and juice)

Bzzz. Bzzz. Bzzz. Jesus loved his disciples. Jesus loves us too.

 **We remember that Jesus loves us.**

Bzzz. Bzzz. Bzzz. Let's say the Bible verse together: "Remember me" (I Corinthians 11:24).

Have the children repeat the Bible verse with BZ Bee.

Have BZ Bee say good-bye to the children. Put the puppet away.

PRESCHOOL: LESSON 2

Choose one or more activities to immerse your children in the Bible story.

Supplies:
CD player

Zillies®:
CD

Praisin' and Singin'

Say: **Jesus wanted his disciples to remember that he loved them. Jesus loves us. We can remember that Jesus loves us as we sing.**

Sing the song "Praisin'," from the **CD (Track 13)**. Do the motions that go along with the song.

Praisin'

Clap, clap! *(Clap hands.)*
Ain't it great to be praisin'
Clap, clap! *(Clap hands.)*
Ain't it great to be praisin',
Praisin' the Lord with all our friends.
Clap, clap! *(Clap hands.)*
Ain't it great to be praisin'..

Stomp, stomp! *(Stomp feet.)*
Ain't it great to be praisin'
Stomp, stomp! *(Stomp feet.)*
Ain't it great to be praisin',
Praisin' the Lord with all our friends.
Stomp, stomp! *(Stomp feet.)*
Ain't it great to be praisin'.
Shake, shake! *(Shake hands with a friend.)*
Ain't it great to be praisin'

Shake, shake! *(Shake hands with a friend.)*
Ain't it great to be praisin',
Praisin' the Lord with all our friends.
Shake, shake! *(Shake hands with a friend.)*
Ain't it great to be praisin'.

Bump, bump! *(Bump hips with a friend.)*
Ain't it great to be praisin'
Bump, bump! *(Bump hips with a friend.)*
Ain't it great to be praisin',
Praisin' the Lord with all our friends.
Bump, bump! *(Bump hips with a friend.)*
Ain't it great to be praisin'.

WORDS: Daphna Flegal
Words © 2001 Abingdon Press

Supplies:
5 items such as a Bible, a pair of scissors, a paintbrush, a crayon, and a CD
a cloth to cover the items

Zillies®:
none

Remembering Game

Ask the children to sit around you in a circle. Show them the items. Place the cloth over the items. Take one away.

Say: **I am going to take the cloth off now. See if you can remember what was there and tell me what is missing.**

Play this several times changing the items that are missing.

Say: **You did very well remembering the things we had covered up. Jesus wants us to remember that he always loves us.**

BibleZone® LIVE

Choose one or more activities to bring the Bible to life.

Jesus Loves Me Pins

Cut hearts out of poster board before class. You can paint the puzzle pieces or let the children paint the puzzle pieces. To create a three-dimensional effect, glue the puzzle pieces to the poster board. Then glue the "Jesus loves me" heart on top of the puzzle pieces. You can attach a safety pin to the back with tape or just use tape to hold the heart on.

Say: Our Bible story taught us Jesus had a special meal with his friends. He told his friends that they should remember him. We can remember that Jesus loves us too. When we wear our pins, they can remind us that Jesus loves us.

Remembering With Ellie

Have the children sit in a circle. Practice signing the Bible verse (I Corinthians 11:24) "Remember me." Do this several times. Place Ellie the Elephant in the middle of the circle.

Say: We're going to play a game with our friend, Ellie the Elephant. I'm going to play music as we pass the rings around the circle. When the music stops, I'll call out a color. If you are holding that color ring, you will put it on Ellie's trunk. Then we'll all sign the Bible verse, "Remember me."

Play this until every child who wants a turn has had a chance.

Supplies:
hearts cut out of posterboard
puzzle pieces painted red
glue
safety pins or tape
smaller heart that says "Jesus Loves Me"

Zillies®:
none

Supplies:
CD player

Zillies®:
inflatable elephant and rings
CD

 **We remember that Jesus loves us.**

PRESCHOOL: LESSON 2

Life

Choose one or more activities to bring the Bible to life.

Supplies:
none

Zillies®:
butterfly fans

Butterfly Prayers:

Have the children sit down in the worship area. Give each child a fan. If you have a large group, you can do this more than once and let them share the fans.

Say: Today we learned about a special meal Jesus had with his friends. Jesus wanted his friends to remember that he loved them. We can remember that Jesus loves us too.

Ask the children to wave their fans in front of them the first three lines of the poem. On the last line, the children will raise their fan and wave it over their head.

> Waving fans can be such fun
> Cool air blows on everyone.
> Wave your fans and let's shout hooray
> We remember Jesus' love today.

Pray: Dear God, Thank you for loving us. Thank you for Jesus. Amen.

Photocopy the HomeZone newsletter to send home to the parents.

 **We remember that Jesus loves us.**

Home Zone For Parents

Bible Verse
Remember me.
I Corinthians 11:24

Bible Story
Matthew 26:17-30
Luke 22:7-23

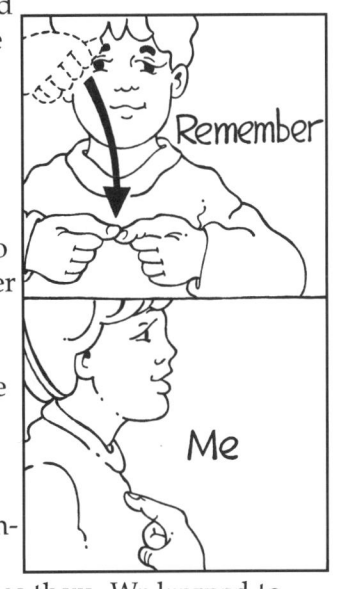

Today we shared the story of Jesus sharing the Last Supper with his friends. Jesus wanted the disciples to remember him when they shared bread and wine. We talked about Jesus wanting his friends to remember that he loved them. We encouraged the children to remember that Jesus loves them. We learned to sign the Bible verse. Ask your child to show you the sign for "Remember me."

Remembering Is Fun

Take some time this week to look through photograph albums or just to recall fun times that you have had. Remember times that you were silly and times that were exciting and times that you just enjoyed being together.

Bake Cookies

You might bake some bread or cookies to share with someone who is sick or unable to get out much. Put a heart note on it that says "Jesus loves you and I do too."

We remember that Jesus loves us.

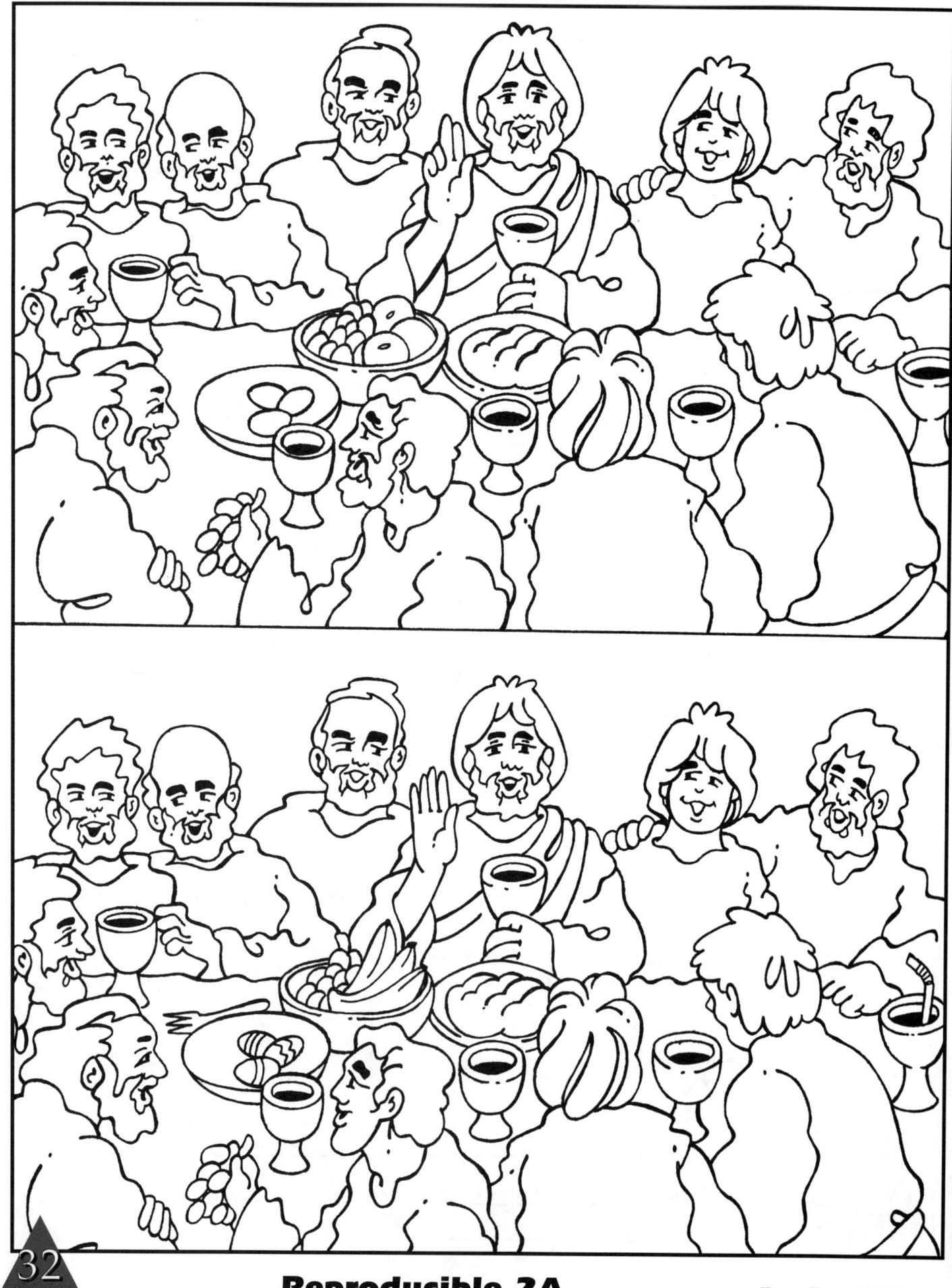

Reproducible 2A

Permission granted to photocopy for local church use. © 2003 Abingdon Press.

BibleZone® LIVE

3 Bible ZONE LIVE

Watch With Me

Enter the Zone

Bible Verse
Jesus went to pray.
(Matthew 26:42)

Bible Story
Matthew 26:36-46; Mark 14:32-42

The Scripture today tells the story of Jesus going to the garden of Gethsemane to pray. He takes three of his disciples with him: Peter, James, and John. Jesus prays, "let this cup pass from me." He knows of the suffering that he must endure and asks God if there is another way. However, each time he prays he always shows his obedience to God by saying that God's will be done.

Jesus asks his friends to watch with him. He doesn't mean that they should watch for the people who are coming to take him away. Jesus is rather asking that they sit with him and be with him in this very trying hour. The disciples instead fall asleep. Jesus comes back to them two times asking them to remain awake, seeking support from his friends. Each time they fall asleep again.

Jesus tells them that they want to do the right thing but they are weak.

With young children, we will focus on the part of the story in which Jesus went to the garden to pray. We need to encourage children to pray. It is good to teach them prayers that they can pray. It is also good to give them opportunities to pray spontaneous prayers. A child should never be forced to pray in front of a group, but should be given the opportunity.

Be sure prayer is a part of your classroom, both for your children and with your children.

God always hears our prayers.

Scope the

ZONE	TIME	SUPPLIES	ZILLIES
Zoom Into the Zone			
Prayer Chain	10 minutes	Reproducible 3A, crayons or markers, paper plate, construction paper, tape, glue, scissors, stapler	none
Decorating the Garden	10 minutes	Transparency 1, tempera paint, green tissue paper, piece of dry wall or a bed sheet, fiberfill, glue	none
BibleZone®			
Praying With Jesus	10 minutes	brown grocery bags, newspaper, tape, crayons	none
Hosanna Hop	3 minutes	none	none
Watch With Me	5 minutes	none	none
Bible Verse Buzz	5 minutes	Bible, BZ Bee	none
Praisin' and Singin'	5 minutes	CD player	CD, rocks made earlier
LifeZone			
Prayer Flowers	5 minutes	cupcake liners, construction paper, large craft sticks, glue, marker	none
Prayer Cards	5 minutes	Reproducible 3B, glue, thick construction paper or posterboard, markers and crayons	none
Remember With Ellie	5 minutes	CD player	inflatable elephant and rings
Butterfly Prayers	3 minutes	none	butterfly fans

Zillies® are found in the **BibleZone® LIVE FUNspirational® Kit.**

PRESCHOOL: LESSON 3

Zoom Into the Zone

Choose one or more activities to capture the attention of your children.

Supplies:
Reproducible 3A
crayons or markers
paper plate
construction paper
  cut into strips,
  7 per child
tape
glue
scissors
stapler

Zillies®:
none

Prayer Chain

Give each child a copy of the poem **(Reproducible 3A)**. Cut out the poem with the picture of Jesus praying. Have the children color the picture. Glue the picture in the center of the paper plate. Put this aside. Show the children how to hook the construction paper strips together to make a chain. Let them tape the chain together. Staple the chain to the paper plate.

Say: Take your prayer chain home. Remember to pray each day. When you pray, you may remove a link of your chain. By the time we meet next, you will have used all of your chain.

Supplies:
Transparency 1
tempera paint (blue
  and green)
green tissue paper
piece of dry wall or a
  bed sheet
fiberfill
glue

Zillies®:
none

Decorating the Garden

Use an overhead projector to trace the garden scene **(Transparency 1)** on a piece of dry wall or on a sheet. Let the children help paint the sky. Add "clumps" of fiberfill to make clouds in the sky. Add a little glue to hold them on, though the wet paint will hold pretty well. Use paint and green tissue paper to make the grass. Stand or hang this in your story area.

Say: Jesus went to the garden with his friends to pray. We're making a garden to use when we hear stories of Jesus in the garden. We will be adding items to our garden each week.

 **God always hears our prayers.**

Choose one or more activities to immerse your children in the Bible story.

Praying With Jesus

Give each child a grocery bag and some pieces of newspaper. Show them how to crumple the newspaper and stuff it in the bag. Continue until the bag is half to three-fourths full. Fold down the top. Let the children help to tape it closed.

Say: In our story today, Jesus went to the garden to pray to God. There were probably rocks in the garden and he might have knelt down by the rock to pray. We will use our rocks when we say a prayer after the story.

Have the children decorate their rocks with crayons.

Take the rocks to the story area and place them near the garden backdrop.

Supplies:
brown grocery bags
newspaper
tape
crayons

Zillies®:
none

Hosanna Hop

Use the "Hosanna Hop" to lead your children to the story area. The children can use the hosanna hoops that they made in Lesson 1.

Hosanna, Hosanna, this is what we say
(Wave hoops overhead in an arc.)
Hosanna, Hosanna, we can shout hooray.
(Jump up in the air, shouting hooray.)
We love to hear the stories that tell us of the way
(Cup hand to ear.)
Jesus taught us how to live and love God everyday.
(Point up and hug self.)
Hosanna, Hosanna, let's stomp on down the road.
(Stomp along.)
Hosanna, Hosanna, let's ride like Jesus rode.
(Pretend to ride donkey.)
Hosanna, Hosanna, let's hop on down the road.
(Hop along.)
Hosanna, Hosanna, let's ride like Jesus rode.
(Pretend to ride donkey.)
Hosanna, Hosanna, this is what we say
(Wave hoops over head in an arc.)
Hosanna, Hosanna, we can shout hooray.
(Jump up in the air, shouting hooray.)

Supplies:
hosanna hoops
 made earlier

Zillies®:
none

PRESCHOOL: LESSON 3

Bible  Story

Watch With Me

by Beth Parr

Have the children sit in a circle. Teach them the refrain to sing to the tune of "Hot Cross Buns."

Pray with me.
Pray with me.
God will always listen, so come
Pray with me.

Jesus went out to the garden of Gethsemane with his friends. He was feeling sad. He wanted to find a quiet place where he could pray to God.

Pray with me.
Pray with me.
God will always listen, so come
Pray with me.

Jesus asked his friends Peter, John, and James to watch with him. He wanted his friends to be with him when he prayed. Jesus walked a little ways from his friends and began to pray to God.

"Father, please be with me. I want to do what you want me to do," Jesus prayed. After Jesus had talked with God for a while, he went back to his friends. They had fallen asleep. Jesus woke them up and asked them again to watch with him.

Pray with me.
Pray with me.
God will always listen, so come
Pray with me.

Then Jesus went back to his prayers. He wanted to obey God. He knew that God always heard his prayers. When Jesus went back to his friends, they were asleep again. This happened one more time.

Jesus was sad that his friends could not stay awake with him. "You say that you want to do the right things but you seem to be weak," said Jesus. This was true. The disciples wanted to do what Jesus asked but they had fallen asleep.

Pray with me.
Pray with me.
God will always listen, so come
Pray with me.

In With BZ Bee

Bible Verse Buzz

Choose a child to hold the Bible open to Matthew 26:42.

Say: Jesus went to the garden to pray. He took his friends with him.

Say the Bible verse, "Jesus went to pray" (Matthew 26:42), for the children. Have the children say the Bible verse after you. Turn your back to the children or hide your hands underneath a table as you place the BZ Bee puppet (see page 174) on your hand. Turn around or bring the puppet out where the children can see it.

Pretend to make the puppet talk. Change your voice for the puppet:

Bzzz, Bzzz, Bzzz. Hi, everybody! I'm BZ Bee.

Bzzz, Bzzz, Bzzz. I like to taste ears. Do you have ears? Yum, yum, yum. Let me taste.

Go to each child. Encourage, but do not force each child to turn his or her ear toward BZ. Have BZ pretend to taste each child's ears. Have BZ say things like:

Mmmm. Mmmm. You taste like honey.
Bzzz. Bzzz. You taste like apples.
Yumm. Yumm. You taste like peaches.

After BZ has tasted each child's ears, **say:**
Bzzz. Bzzz. Bzzz. I like to taste your ears. They're yummy. *(Rub BZ's stomach.)*

Bzzz. Bzzz. Bzzz. I like something else even more than ears. I like the Bible.
Bzzz. Bzzz. Bzzz. You heard a Bible story today. Why did Jesus go to the garden? *(to pray)* **Who went with him?** *(his friends or Peter, James, and John)* **What did Jesus' friends do?** *(fell asleep)* **Who did Jesus pray to?** *(God)*

Bzzz. Bzzz. Bzzz. God listened to Jesus' prayers. God listens to our prayers too.

God always hears our prayers.

Bzzz. Bzzz. Bzzz. Let's say the Bible verse together: "Jesus went to pray" (Matthew 26:42).

Have the children repeat the Bible verse with BZ Bee.

Have BZ Bee say good-bye to the children. Put the puppet away.

Preschool: Lesson 3

Bible

Choose one or more activities to immerse your children in the Bible story.

Supplies:
CD player
rocks made earlier

Zillies®:
CD

Praisin' and Singin'

Say: Jesus went to the garden to pray. His friends went with him. God listened to Jesus when he prayed. God always hears our prayers. Let's sing a song about our story.

Sing the song, "Garden of Gethsemane" using the instrumental tune, "Are You Sleeping" from the **CD (Track 15)**. Let the children pretend to sleep with their heads propped on their rocks. Stretch to wake up. Kneel by rocks to pray.

> Are you sleeping?
> Are you sleeping?
> *(Pretend to sleep with head on rock.)*
> My good friends?
> My good friends?
> *(Hold your hands over your heart.)*
> Now it's time to wake up!
> Now it's time to wake up!
> *(Stretch arms over head.)*
> Pray with me.
> Pray with me.
> *(Kneel by rocks.)*
>
> Based on Matthew 26:36-46
> WORDS: Sharilyn S. Adair, Lora Jean Gowan, and Linda Ray Miller
> Words © 2000 Cokesbury

Repeat as children enjoy it.

 **God always hears our prayers.**

BibleZone® LIVE

Choose one or more activities to bring the Bible to life.

Prayer Flowers

Give each child a piece of construction paper and a cupcake liner. Have them glue the cupcake liner in the middle of their construction paper. Give each child four or five craft stick pieces. Ask them to tell you things they would like to thank God for. You may need to make some suggestions: my family, food, my friends, and so forth.

Write their answers on the craft sticks—one to a stick. Have them glue these around the cupcake liner to make a flower.

Say: Our Bible story taught us Jesus prayed to God. We can pray to God. One way we can pray is to thank God for special things. You've put some of those special things on your flowers.

Pray: Dear God, thank you for loving us. Thank you for all these special people and blessings in our lives. Amen.

Supplies:
cupcake liners
construction paper
large craft sticks (cut in half)
glue
marker

Zillies®:
none

Prayer Cards

Give each child a copy of the prayer card **(Reproducible 3B)** Let them color the picture and decorate the borders. Glue this to the heavier paper. Fold in half so that it will stand.

Say: This is a prayer card you can put on your table at home to remind you to pray before you eat. It has a blessing on it that you can use or you may want to say a blessing you already know.

Supplies:
Reproducible 3B
glue
thick construction paper or posterboard
markers and crayons

Zillies®:
none

PRESCHOOL: LESSON 3

Choose one or more activities to bring the Bible to life.

Supplies:
CD Player

Zillies®:
inflatable elephant and rings
CD

Remember With Ellie

Have the children sit in a circle. Place Ellie the Elephant in the middle of the circle.

Say: We're going to play a game with our friend, Ellie the Elephant. I'm going to play music as we pass the rings around the circle. When the music stops, I'll call out a color. If you are holding that color ring, you will put it on Ellie's trunk. Then we'll all say the Bible verse, "Jesus went to pray."

Play this until every child who wants a turn has had a chance.

Supplies:
none

Zillies®:
butterfly fans

Butterfly Prayers:

Have the children sit down in the worship area. Give each child a fan. If you have a large group, you can do this more than once and let them share the fans.

Say: Today we learned about that Jesus prayed to God. Jesus knew that God would listen. We can pray to God. God always hears our prayers.

Ask the children to wave their fans in front of them the first three lines of the poem. On the last line, the children will raise their fan and wave it over their head.

> Waving fans can be such fun
> Cool air blows on everyone.
> Wave your fans and let's shout hooray
> We remember God hears us pray.

Pray: Dear God, Thank you for loving us. Thank you for always listening to our prayers. Amen.

Photocopy the HomeZone newsletter to send home to the parents.

BibleZone® LIVE

Home Zone For Parents

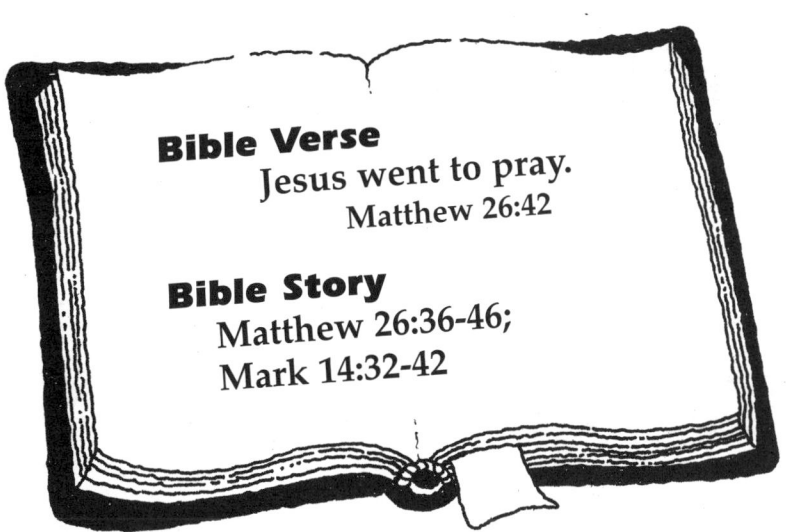

Bible Verse
Jesus went to pray.
Matthew 26:42

Bible Story
Matthew 26:36-46;
Mark 14:32-42

Today we shared the story of Jesus praying in the Garden of Gethsemane. Jesus took his disciples with him. He asked them to watch with him. He was not asking them to watch for those who were coming to get him. He was asking them to be with him and support him. Jesus' disciples fell asleep. Jesus woke them up three times, but each time they fell asleep.

For young children, we have focused on Jesus praying to God. Jesus knew that God would listen to him. We shared with the children that God always hears our prayers.

Sing Along Song

The children learned a special song today. It can be sung to the tune of "Hot Cross Buns." Sing this song with your child at mealtime or at bedtime when they say their prayers.

> Pray with me.
> Pray with me.
> God will always listen, so
> come pray with me.

Enjoy singing together.

God always hears our prayers.

Jesus taught us all to pray.
We can pray on every day.
We know that God will always hear.
We know that God is always near.
Each day when to God I pray
I will take one loop away.

Reproducible 3A

God is great.

God is good.

Let us thank him for our food.

Amen.

PRESCHOOL: LESSON 3

Reproducible 3B

Permission granted to photocopy for local church use. © 2003 Abingdon Press.

4 Bible LIVE

I Don't Know Him

Enter the Zone

Bible Verse
Right then a rooster crowed.
(John 18:27)

Bible Story
Luke 22:54-62; John 18:15-18, 25-27

The Scripture today tells the story of Peter's denial of Jesus. Earlier, Jesus had told Peter that he would deny knowing him three times before the rooster crowed. Peter had protested greatly. He told Jesus that there was no way that he would ever deny knowing Jesus. Yet in the aftermath of Jesus' arrest, Peter was frightened and quickly forgot his own words. Peter was waiting outside the high priest's house to hear what had happened to Jesus. Three different people asked him if he was a follower of Jesus. Each time he denied it. The sound of the rooster crowing made Peter remember Jesus' words. He was heartbroken that he had denied knowing Jesus.

Peter had the opportunity each time to affirm his belief in Jesus and to testify to his faith. He was afraid and too weak to respond. Jesus knew that this would happen. The rooster provided the reminder for Peter of who he was and to whom he belonged. Though he was devastated by his own weakness, Peter would still continue to grow and to be the leader of the church that Jesus knew he could be.

Preschoolers will not understand all the implications of this story in terms of the questioning of Jesus by Jewish authorities. We will not explore the whole story. Our focus will be on the fact that the rooster crowing reminded Peter that Jesus was his friend. They can appreciate that Jesus is always their friend.

We know that Jesus is always our friend.

Scope the Zone

ZONE	TIME	SUPPLIES	ZILLIES
Zoom Into the Zone			
My Friend Jesus	10 minutes	Reproducible 4A, crayons or markers, white vinegar, small bowls, heart shapes cut from red tissue paper, paintbrushes	none
Decorating the Garden	10 minutes	Transparency 1, scraps of black and gray construction paper, glue	none
BibleZone			
Crowing for Friends	10 minutes	Reproducible 4B, cardboard paper roll, glue, tempera paint, paintbrushes, tape	none
Hosanna Hop	3 minutes	hosanna hoops	none
I Don't Know Him	5 minutes	rooster puppet made earlier	none
Bible Verse Buzz	5 minutes	Bible, BZ Bee	none
Praisin' and Singin'	5 minutes	CD player	CD
LifeZone			
Friendship Book	5 minutes	white paper, construction paper, crayons or markers, instant camera with film, brads, paper punch, glue	none
Friendship Bracelets	5 minutes	construction paper; construction paper hearts or heart stickers; wide, clear packing tape; Velcro; glue; masking tape	none
Remembering With Friends	5 minutes	CD Player	CD

Zillies® are found in the **BibleZone® LIVE FUNspirational® Kit.**

PRESCHOOL: LESSON 4

Zoom Into the Zone

Choose one or more activities to capture the attention of your children.

Supplies:
Reproducible 4A
crayons or markers
white vinegar
small bowls
heart shapes cut from red tissue paper (don't use the fade resistant kind)
paintbrushes

Zillies®:
none

My Friend Jesus

Give each child a copy of the picture of Jesus **(Reproducible 4A)**. Have the children color the picture of Jesus. Pour the vinegar into bowls. Give each child a paintbrush. Have the children brush the vinegar all around the picture of Jesus. Give them the tissue paper hearts to put all over their paper. When the vinegar dries, the tissue hearts will fall off, leaving heart prints on the paper.

Caution: Fade-resistant paper will not work.

This picture will be used later in the lesson to create the children's Friendship Book.

 **We know that Jesus is always our friend.**

Supplies:
scraps of colored black and gray construction paper
glue
Transparency 1

Zillies®:
none

Decorating the Garden

Use the garden scene that you traced in lesson 3 **(Transparency 1)**. Stand or hang this in your story area. Let the children use scraps of black and gray colored construction paper to make stones to put in the garden.

Say: We're making a garden to use when we hear stories of Jesus in the garden. Every garden has stones. Today we will put some stones in our garden.

BibleZone® LIVE

Choose one or more activities to immerse your children in the Bible story.

Crowing for Friends

Copy the rooster puppet **(Reproducible 4B)** for each child. Have the children paint the rooster and the tail feathers. After they are finished, let the children help you attach the rooster to the cardboard tube or a rolled piece of paper with tape. Later, the children will use their puppet to tell the story.

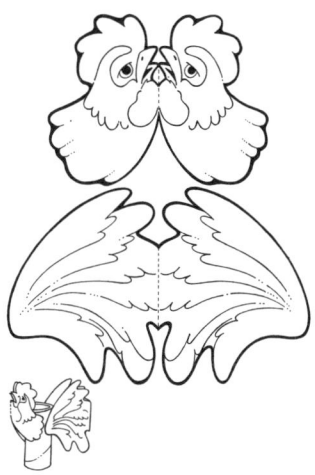

Supplies:
Reproducible 4B (1 per child)
cardboard paper roll, 1 per child
glue
tempera paint
paintbrushes
tape

Zillies®:
none

Hosanna Hop

Use the "Hosanna Hop" to lead your children to the story area. The children can use the hosanna hoops that they made in Lesson 1.

Hosanna, Hosanna, this is what we say
(Wave hoops overhead in an arc.)
Hosanna, Hosanna, we can shout hooray.
(Jump up in the air, shouting hooray.)
We love to hear the stories that tell us of the way
(Cup hand to ear.)
Jesus taught us how to live and love God everyday.
(Point up and hug self.)
Hosanna, Hosanna, let's stomp on down the road.
(Stomp along.)
Hosanna, Hosanna, let's ride like Jesus rode.
(Pretend to ride donkey.)
Hosanna, Hosanna, let's hop on down the road.
(Hop along.)
Hosanna, Hosanna, let's ride like Jesus rode.
(Pretend to ride donkey.)
Hosanna, Hosanna, this is what we say
(Wave hoops over head in an arc.)
Hosanna, Hosanna, we can shout hooray.
(Jump up in the air, shouting hooray.)

Supplies:
hosanna hoops (Lesson 1)

Zillies®:
none

Bible  Story

I Don't Know Him

by Beth Parr

Have the children sit in a circle. Ask the children to help you tell the story with their rooster puppets.

Say: Let's practice. How does a rooster sound? *(Let the children practice crowing.)* **That was great. Now we're ready to start. Be sure to have your rooster ready to crow.**

Hurry, hurry, hurry! *(Pat hands on thigh.)* Some men took Jesus to the house of the high priest to ask him questions. They were angry with Jesus. Peter hurried to follow them and stood outside the house. He hoped to find out what was going on.

Shiver, shiver, shiver. *(Rub arms and shiver.)* Peter was very cold and frightened. He saw that the servants who worked in the house had built a fire outside to keep warm. Peter walked up to the fire and began to warm his hands. It felt so good not to be cold anymore.

Looking, Looking, Looking. *(Shade eyes and look around.)* A woman standing by the fire looked at Peter. She said, "Aren't you one of Jesus' friends?"

No, No, No. *(Shake head.)* "I am not a friend of Jesus. I don't even know him."

Looking, Looking, Looking. *(Shade eyes and look around.)* A man standing by the fire looked at Peter. He said, "Aren't you one of Jesus' friends?"

No, No, No. *(Shake head.)* "I am not a friend of Jesus."

Looking, Looking, Looking. *(Shade eyes and look around.)* A while later another man said, "Aren't you one of Jesus' friends? You're from the same town of Galilee."

No, No, No. *(Shake head.)* "I don't know what you are talking about. Jesus is not my friend."

Crow, Crow, Crow. *(Raise puppets and crow.)* Crow, Crow, Crow. *(Raise puppets and crow.)* Peter heard the rooster crow. The sound of the rooster crowing helped Peter remember that Jesus was his friend.

Crow, Crow, Crow. *(Raise puppets and crow.)* Peter remembered that Jesus was his friend.

BIBLEZONE® LIVE

In With BZ Bee

Bible Verse Buzz

Choose a child to hold the Bible open to John 18:27.

Say: Peter told people that Jesus was not his friend. When the rooster crowed, he remembered that Jesus was his friend.

Say the Bible verse, "Right then a rooster crowed" (John 18:27), for the children. Have the children say the Bible verse after you. Turn your back to the children or hide your hands underneath a table as you place the BZ Bee puppet (see page 174) on your hand. Turn around or bring the puppet out where the children can see it.

Pretend to make the puppet talk. Change your voice for the puppet:

Bzzz, Bzzz, Bzzz. Hi, everybody! I'm BZ Bee.

Bzzz, Bzzz, Bzzz. I like to taste ears. Do you have ears? Yum, yum, yum. Let me taste.

Go to each child. Encourage, but do not force each child to turn his or her ear toward BZ. Have BZ pretend to taste each child's ears. Have BZ say things like:

Mmmm. Mmmm. You taste like honey.
Bzzz. Bzzz. You taste like apples.
Yumm. Yumm. You taste like peaches.

After BZ has tasted each child's ears, **say:**
Bzzz. Bzzz. Bzzz. I like to taste your ears. They're yummy. (Rub BZ's stomach.)

Bzzz. Bzzz. Bzzz. I like something else even more than ears. I like the Bible.

Bzzz. Bzzz. Bzzz. You heard a Bible story today. What did Peter tell the people who asked him if he knew Jesus? (I don't know him; he's not my friend.) **When the rooster crowed, what did Peter remember?** (Jesus was his friend.)

Bzzz. Bzzz. Bzzz. The crowing of the rooster helped Peter remember that Jesus was his friend. We can remember that Jesus is our friend.

We know that Jesus is always our friend.

Bzzz. Bzzz. Bzzz. Let's say the Bible verse together: "Right then a rooster crowed" (John 18:27).

Have the children repeat the Bible verse with BZ Bee.

Have BZ Bee say good-bye to the children. Put the puppet away.

Preschool: Lesson 4

Choose one or more activities to immerse your children in the Bible story.

Supplies:
CD player

Zillies®:
CD

Praisin' and Singin'

Say: The crowing of the rooster helped Peter remember that Jesus was his friend. Jesus is our friend. Let's sing a song about our friend Jesus.

Sing the song, "My Best Friend Is Jesus," from the **CD (Track 6)**.

My best friend is Jesus. Love him, love him.
My best friend is Jesus. I love him.
My best friend is Jesus. Serve him, serve him.
My best friend is Jesus. I serve him.
My best friend is Jesus. Thank him, thank him.
My best friend is Jesus. I thank him.

©1939, 1967, 1993 Broadman Press. Distributed by Genevox Music Group. Used by permission.

BibleZone® LIVE

Choose one or more activities to bring the Bible to life.

Friendship Book

Move the chairs from the table. Write the name of each child at the top of a piece of paper. You will need to do this as many times as there are children in your class. Place one set of the papers all around the table. Have the children draw a picture of themselves, trace their handprint, and/or write their name. Collect these papers and do it again. Do it as many times as it takes to make a friendship book for each child. Take a picture of the group, one for each child. Let them glue these pictures to a page.
The last page will be the "My Friend Jesus" picture they made earlier. Punch holes in the pages. Let the children help you put brads into the book.

Say: In our story today, Peter remembered that Jesus was his friend when he heard the rooster crow. We know that Jesus is always our friend. We also have friends who are here with us today. We've made a book so that we can remember our friends.

Supplies:
white paper
construction paper
crayons or markers
instant camera with film
brads
paper punch
glue

Zillies®:
none

Friendship Bracelets

Give each child a strip of construction paper and several hearts. Let them glue or stick the hearts on the construction paper. Cut a length of tape the same length as the construction paper. Lay the construction paper bracelet face down on the sticky side. Fold the end over. Attach small pieces of Velcro to close the bracelet or use masking tape.

Say: We know that Jesus is always our friend. We can wear our bracelets so that others will know that Jesus is our friend.

Supplies:
strips of construction paper (about 1-inch wide) to fit around child's wrist, 1 per child
hearts cut out of construction paper or heart stickers, 1 heart per child that says Jesus is my friend
wide, clear packing tape
Velcro
glue
masking tape

Zillies®:
none

PRESCHOOL: LESSON 4

Life Zone

Choose one or more activities to bring the Bible to life.

Supplies:
CD player

Zillies®:
2 plastic baskets and 3 Easter eggs
CD

Remembering With Friends

Have the children stand in a line. Give the child at one end of the line the yellow basket with the three eggs in it.

Give the purple basket to the child at the other end.

Say: We're going to play a game. We will have to work together with our friends. I am going to play some music while we pass the eggs down the line. _____ (child's name) **will take an egg out of the yellow basket and pass it down the line. When the egg reaches the end,** _____ (child's name) **will put it in the purple basket. Then we'll all say our Bible verse, "right then a rooster crowed." Then we'll pass another egg and then another. When we have all three eggs in the purple basket, let's shout, "Hooray, Jesus is our friend."**

You can play this several times changing the children at the beginning and the end of the line.

Supplies:
none

Zillies®:
butterfly fans

Butterfly Prayers

Have the children sit down in the worship area. Give each child a fan. If you have a large group, you can do this more than once and let them share the fans.

Say: Today we learned that when Peter heard the rooster crow, he remembered Jesus was his friend. We know that Jesus is always our friend.

Ask the children to wave their fans in front of them the first three lines of the poem. On the last line the children will raise their fan and wave it over their head.

> Waving fans can be such fun
> Cool air blows on everyone.
> Wave your fans and let's shout hooray
> We remember our friend Jesus. Yea!

Pray: Dear God, Thank you for giving us Jesus as such a special friend. Thank you for our friends we love to play with. Amen.

Photocopy the HomeZone newsletter to send home to the parents.

BibleZone® LIVE

Home Zone For Parents

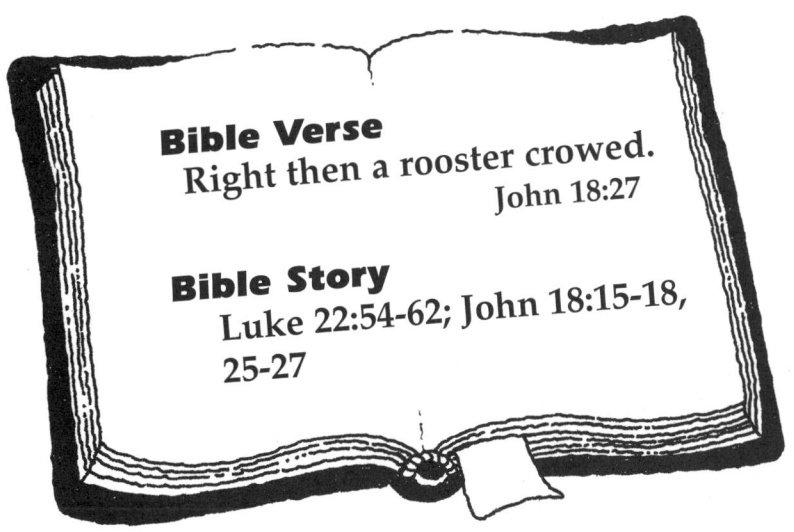

Bible Verse
Right then a rooster crowed.
John 18:27

Bible Story
Luke 22:54-62; John 18:15-18, 25-27

Today we shared the story of Peter's denial of Jesus. Our story told of Peter telling three different people that he didn't know Jesus. When the rooster crowed, Peter remembered that Jesus was his friend. All of the circumstances surrounding Peter's denial are really too difficult for young children to understand. They can understand about friends. We know that Jesus is always our friend. We have other friends that we like to play with. Preschoolers sometimes have trouble sharing and playing with their friends. Encourage your child to be a good friend. Invite a friend over to play this week.

Cut out the finger puppets here. Cut out the finger holes. Color these with your children. Enjoy telling stories with your puppet friends.

We know that Jesus is always our friend.

PRESCHOOL: LESSON 4   Permission granted to photocopy for local church use. © 2003 Abingdon Press.

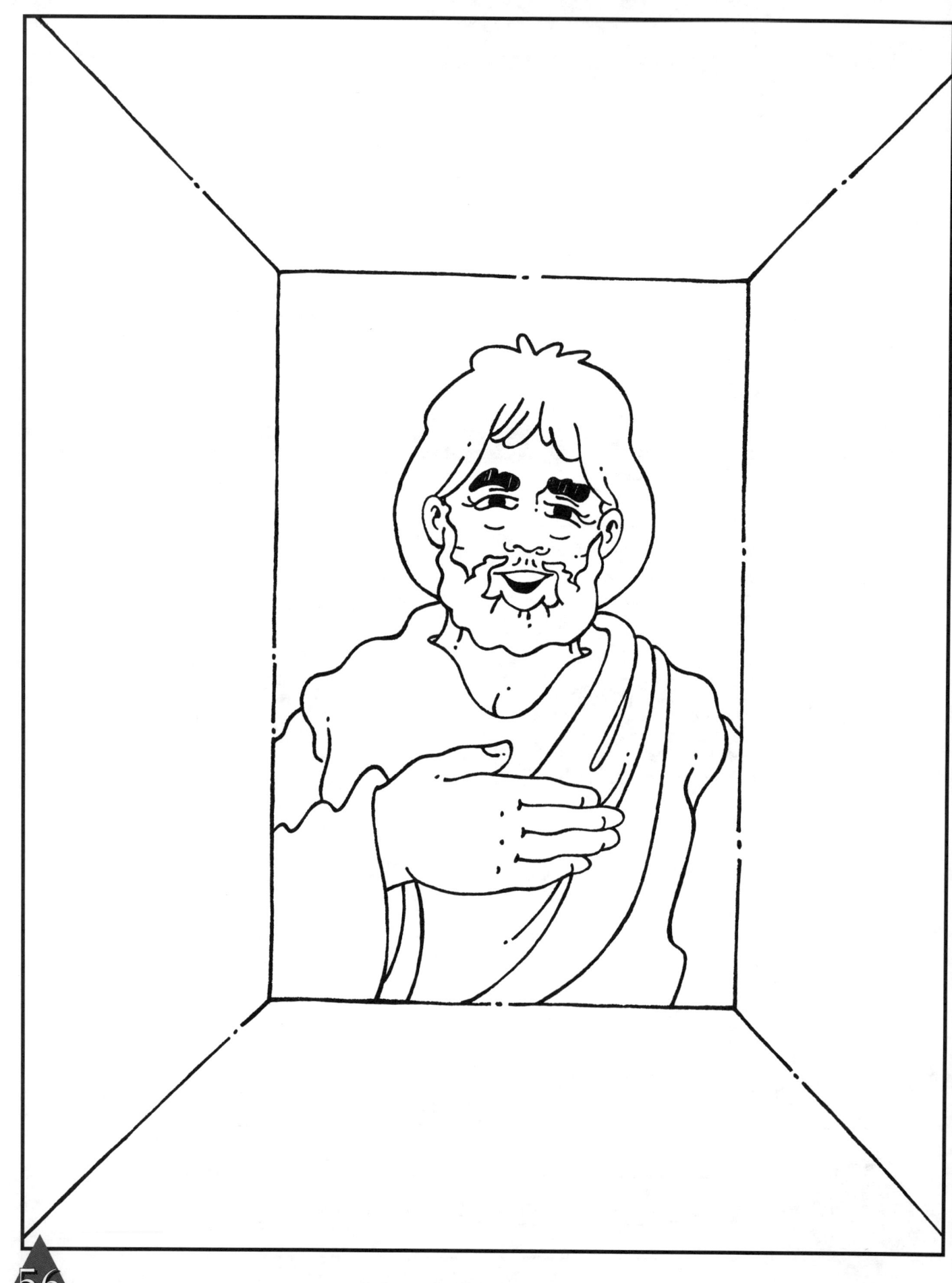

Reproducible 4A

Permission granted to photocopy for local church use. © 2003 Abingdon Press.

Preschool: Lesson 4 — **Reproducible 4B**
Permission granted to photocopy for local church use. © 2003 Abingdon Press.

5 Bible Zone LIVE

The Garden Tomb

Enter the Zone

Bible Verse
This man really was God's Son!
(Matthew 27:54)

Bible Story
Luke 23:44-56; John 19:38-42

The Scripture today deals with the death and burial of Jesus. The sky grew dark in the middle of the day. The whole atmosphere conveyed the magnitude of what was happening. The sun stopped shining and the curtain in the temple split. Jesus spoke, committing himself into God's hands, and then died. All they had seen overwhelmed the people. They sadly returned home. Jesus' close friends stood at a distance and watched.

Joseph of Arimathea, who is characterized as a good man, asked for Jesus' body. Joseph was part of the Sanhedrin but he did not agree with the decision that had been made. He wrapped Jesus' body in fine linen and put it in a garden tomb just before the Sabbath began.

Under Jewish law, the burial had to take place before the Sabbath began because Jews could not work on the Sabbath day. The women who were with the disciples saw the tomb and how Jesus' body was laid inside the tomb. They went to their homes to prepare the spices and ointments they would bring after the Sabbath. In obedience to God's law, they rested on the Sabbath day. Touching a dead body would have made them ritually unclean, so the necessary rituals could not take place until after the Sabbath.

The response of the Roman soldiers to all that had happened was that this man Jesus was really a good man, truly the Son of God. The soldiers recognized that this was no ordinary man. They knew that they had witnessed a monumental event.

This part of the Easter story will be very difficult for young children to understand. As we talk about Jesus being buried in the tomb, they may recall a grandparent who has died. They may want to share information about that with the class. They may want to know why Jesus rose from the dead and their grandparent did not. Our answers need not exceed their ability or our ability to understand. We can simply answer that we can't always understand what has happened. Assure the child that God loves and will take care of their grandparent. Our focus will be on the affirmation that Jesus was really God's Son. Just like all who were present at the tomb, we know that Jesus is the Son of God.

We know that Jesus is God's Son.

Scope the ZONE

ZONE	TIME	SUPPLIES	ZILLIES
Zoom Into the Zone			
Colorful Crosses	10 minutes	Reproducible 5A, paintbrushes or cotton swabs, pieces of foil, wrapping paper, glue, glitter, yarn or ribbon, paper punch, scissors	none
Decorating the Garden	10 minutes	coffee filters, watercolor markers, ice, plastic sheeting	none
BibleZone®			
In the Darkness	10 minutes	white construction paper, white crayons, black paint paintbrushes	none
Hosanna Hop	3 minutes	hosanna hoops	none
The Garden Tomb	5 minutes	none	none
Bible Verse Buzz	3 minutes	Bible, BZ Bee	none
Flowers for the Garden	5 minutes	coffee filters (colored earlier), chenille stems, masking tape	none
Praisin' and Singin'	5 minutes	CD player	CD
LifeZone			
Remembering God's Son	5 minutes	Reproducible 5B, crayons or markers, tape, scissors	none
Remembering With Friends	5 minutes	CD player	plastic baskets, eggs, CD
Butterfly Prayers	4 minutes	none	butterfly fans

Zillies® are found in the **BibleZone**® **LIVE FUNspirational**® **Kit.**

PRESCHOOL: LESSON 5

Zoom Into the Zone

Choose one or more activities to capture the attention of your children.

Supplies:
Reproducible 5A
paintbrushes or cotton swabs
pieces of foil wrapping paper
glue
glitter
yarn or ribbon
paper punch
scissors

Zillies®:
none

Colorful Crosses

Give each child a cross cut from **Reproducible 5A**. Punch a hole in the top of the cross. Have the children "paint" the cross with glue using paintbrushes or cotton swabs. Place the pieces of foil all over the cross. Then paint lightly with glue again. Sprinkle glitter all over the cross. If you do this with a kitchen shaker and place the cross in a shirt box, it will be less messy and you can reuse some of the glitter.

Say: Our beautiful crosses remind us of Jesus. Jesus loves us.

 **We know that Jesus is God's Son.**

Supplies:
coffee filters
watercolor markers
ice
chenille stems
plastic sheeting to cover table

Zillies®:
none

Decorating the Garden

Say: Today we are going to make flowers to add to our garden scene.

Give each child a coffee filter. Encourage them to color all over the filter with the watercolor markers. When they have finished coloring, give them a piece of ice to rub all over the filter. This will cause the colors to run together and make beautiful flowers.

Tip: If you freeze water in small (three-ounce) paper cups, you can tear away some of the cup and this will give the children a holder for their ice. The colors will get on their hands but they do come off.

Put these aside to dry. The chenille stems will be added to the flowers later.

Say: We're making a garden to use when we hear stories of Jesus in the garden. We will add our flowers to the garden during our story.

Bible

Choose one or more activities to immerse your children in the Bible story.

In the Darkness

Before class draw a cross on each paper with the white crayon. Give each child a piece of paper.

Say: On the day when Jesus died, it became very dark. The people were very sad. Let's paint our pictures with dark paint. There's a surprise in your picture.

Have the children paint the whole page with black paint. The cross that was drawn will stand out in the paint.

Say: The people with Jesus were very sad when he died. The cross reminds us that God sent his Son Jesus because God loves us very much. God is always with us.

Supplies:
white construction or drawing paper
white crayons
black paint
paintbrushes

Zillies®:
none

Hosanna Hop

Use the "Hosanna Hop" to lead your children to the story area. The children can use the hosanna hoops that they made in Lesson 1.

Hosanna, Hosanna, this is what we say
(Wave hoops overhead in an arc)
Hosanna, Hosanna, we can shout hooray.
(Jump up in the air, shouting hooray)
We love to hear the stories that tell us of the way
(Cup hand to ear)
Jesus taught us how to live and love God everyday.
(Point up and hug self)
Hosanna, Hosanna, let's stomp on down the road.
(Stomp along)
Hosanna, Hosanna, let's ride like Jesus rode.
(Pretend to ride donkey.)
Hosanna, Hosanna, let's hop on down the road.
(Hop along)
Hosanna, Hosanna, let's ride like Jesus rode.
(Pretend to ride donkey.)
Hosanna, Hosanna, this is what we say
(Wave hoops over head in an arc)
Hosanna, Hosanna, we can shout hooray.
(Jump up in the air, shouting hooray.)

Supplies:
hosanna hoops made earlier

Zillies®:
none

PRESCHOOL: LESSON 5

 Bible Zone Story

The Garden Tomb

by Beth Parr

Have the children sit in a circle. Invite the children to add their flowers to the garden scene. You can tape them on or have Styrofoam for them to stick the flowers in. Ask the children to join in the refrain:

*Jesus was special to everyone.
We know Jesus is God's own Son.*

The sky was getting very, very dark in the middle of the day. The sun had stopped shining. Everyone was feeling very sad because Jesus had died.

Jesus was special to everyone.
We know Jesus is God's own Son.

The soldiers saw all that had happened. One of the soldiers said, "Jesus must really have been a good man!" (Luke 23:47, CEV). Another soldier said that now he knew that Jesus really was God's Son.

Jesus was special to everyone.
We know Jesus is God's own Son.

A kind man named Joseph took Jesus' body down from the cross. He wrapped it in very fine cloth. He put Jesus' body in a tomb in the garden. Joseph knew that Jesus was God's Son.

Jesus was special to everyone.
We know Jesus is God's own Son.

A man named Nicodemus brought some sweet-smelling spices. Nicodemus loved Jesus. He knew that Jesus was God's Son.

Jesus was special to everyone.
We know Jesus is God's own Son.

There were women who came to the garden tomb to make sure everything was right. They planned to come back on the next day. They knew that Jesus was God's Son.

Jesus was special to everyone.
We know Jesus is God's own Son.

In With BZ Bee

Bible Verse Buzz

Choose a child to hold the Bible open to Matthew 27:54.

Say: A soldier who was there when Jesus died saw everything that had happened and knew that Jesus was God's Son.

Say the Bible verse, "This man really was God's Son!" (Matthew 27:54), for the children. Have the children say the Bible verse after you.

Turn your back to the children or hide your hands underneath a table as you place the BZ Bee puppet (see page 174) on your hand. Turn around or bring the puppet out where the children can see it.

Pretend to make the puppet talk. Change your voice for the puppet:

Bzzz, Bzzz, Bzzz. Hi, everybody! I'm BZ Bee.

Bzzz, Bzzz, Bzzz. I like to taste ears. Do you have ears? Yum, yum, yum. Let me taste.

Go to each child. Encourage, but do not force each child to turn his or her ear toward BZ. Have BZ pretend to taste each child's ears. Have BZ say things like:

**Mmmm. Mmmm. You taste like honey.
Bzzz. Bzzz. You taste like apples.
Yumm. Yumm. You taste like peaches.**

After BZ has tasted each child's ears, **say:
Bzzz. Bzzz. Bzzz. I like to taste your ears. They're yummy.** (Rub BZ's stomach.)

Bzzz. Bzzz. Bzzz. I like something else even more than ears. I like the Bible.

Bzzz. Bzzz. Bzzz. You heard a Bible story today. What did the soldier say about Jesus? (Jesus is God's Son.) **Where did Joseph put Jesus' body after he died?** (in the garden tomb)

Bzzz. Bzzz. Bzzz. The soldier and Joseph and Nicodemus and the women all knew that Jesus was the Son of God. Jesus is God's Son.

We know that Jesus is God's Son.

Bzzz. Bzzz. Bzzz. Let's say the Bible verse together: "This man really was God's Son!" (Matthew 27:54).

Have the children repeat the Bible verse with BZ Bee.

Have BZ Bee say good-bye to the children. Put the puppet away.

PRESCHOOL: LESSON 5

Choose one or more activities to immerse your children in the Bible story.

Supplies:
coffee filters that were colored earlier
chenille stems
masking tape

Zillies®:
none

Supplies:
CD player

Zillies®:
CD

Flowers for the Garden

Give the children their colored coffee filter. Show them how to grab it in the middle to bunch it like a flower. Wrap one end of the chenille stem around the end of the filter to make a stem. Attach the flowers to the garden scene with masking tape.

Praisin' and Singin'

Say: Jesus is God's Son and Jesus is our friend. Let's sing our song about our friend Jesus.

Sing the song, "My Best Friend is Jesus," from the **CD (Track 6)**.

My best friend is Jesus. Love him, love him.
My best friend is Jesus. I love him.
My best friend is Jesus. Serve him, serve him.
My best friend is Jesus. I serve him.
My best friend is Jesus. Thank him, thank him.
My best friend is Jesus. I thank him.

©1939, 1967, 1993 Broadman Press. Distributed by Genevox Music Group. Used by permission.

BibleZone® LIVE

Choose one or more activities to bring the Bible to life.

Remembering God's Son

Supplies:
Reproducible 5B
crayons or markers
tape
scissors

Zillies®:
none

Copy the suns (**Reproducible 5B**) before class. Give each child a copy.

Have them color the two suns on the page.

Help the children cut out the suns and place loops of tape on the back of each sun. Have the children join you in a circle on one side of the room. Explain the game to them.

Say: We're going to play a little game to remind us that Jesus is God's Son. When I call your name, I will tell you how to move. Take one of your suns and tape it to the wall somewhere in our room. Then we'll all say the Bible Verse. Let's practice our Bible verse once. "This man really was God's Son!" (Matthew 27:54).

Call the child by name.

Say: _____(child's name) **hop to the wall with your sun. Let's say the Bible verse.**

Each child can have two turns if you have time. If you have a large class, you may want to send two or three children at a time.

Say: We know that Jesus is God's Son. Let's sing a song to remember that Jesus is God's Son. Sing "God's Son" to the tune of "The Farmer in the Dell."

> Oh, Jesus is God's Son,
> Oh, Jesus is God's Son,
> Hi, ho, we're glad we know
> That Jesus is God's Son.

PRESCHOOL: LESSON 5

Life Zone

Choose one or more activities to bring the Bible to life.

Supplies:
CD player

Zillies®:
2 plastic baskets and 3 Easter eggs
CD

Remembering With Friends

Have the children stand in a line. Give the child at one end of the line the yellow basket with the three eggs in it.

Give the purple basket to the child at the other end.

Say: We're going to play a game. We will have to work together with our friends. I am going to play some music while we pass the eggs down the line. _____ (child's name) **will take an egg out of the yellow basket and pass it down the line. When the egg reaches the end, _____** (child's name) **will put it in the purple basket. Then we'll all say our Bible verse; "This man really was God's Son!" Then we'll pass another egg and then another. When we have all three eggs in the basket, let's shout "Hooray, Jesus is God's Son!"**

You can play this several times changing the children at the beginning and end of the line.

Supplies:
none

Zillies®:
butterfly fans

Butterfly Prayers:

Have the children sit down in the worship area. Give each child a fan. If you have a large group, you can do this more than once and let them share the fans.

Say: Today we learned that the soldier, Joseph, Nicodemus, and the women all knew that Jesus was God's Son. We know that Jesus is God's Son.

Ask the children to wave their fans in front of them the first three lines of the poem. On the last line, everyone raises their fan and waves it over their head.

> Waving fans can be such fun
> Cool air blows on everyone.
> Wave your fans and let's shout hooray
> We remember God' Son Jesus. Yea!

Pray: Dear God, Thank you for your Son Jesus. Thank you for always taking care of us. Amen.

Photocopy the HomeZone newsletter to send home to the parents.

Home Zone For Parents

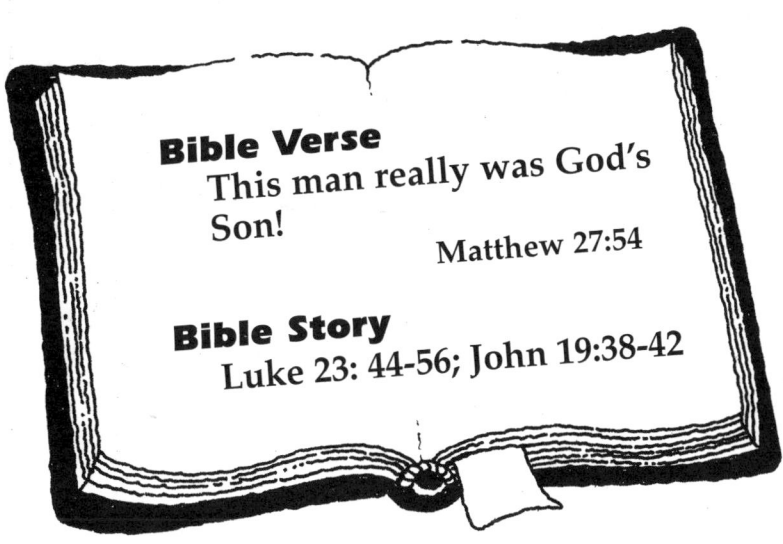

Bible Verse
This man really was God's Son!
Matthew 27:54

Bible Story
Luke 23: 44-56; John 19:38-42

Today we shared the story of the death and burial of Jesus. The story of the crucifixion is too difficult for young children. We emphasized the fact that the people who saw all that had happened that day knew that Jesus was God's Son. We played games to remind us of our Bible verse today. As we prepare for Easter this week, take time to read some Easter stories with your child. Plan some special Easter fun—baking, hiding eggs, or taking a small gift to someone who is homebound.

Edible Easter Baskets

Have fun making, eating and sharing these Easter baskets.

You will need:
- canned biscuits or biscuit mix
- spray oil
- ribbon (cut in 7-inch lengths)
- muffin tin

Turn the muffin tin upside down and spray with the oil. Pat the biscuit flat and mold over the muffin tins. Bake according to package directions. When you first take the pan out of the oven, poke holes on either side of the basket for handles. After the baskets have cooled completely, add ribbons for handles. Fill with jellybeans, raisins, or trail mix.

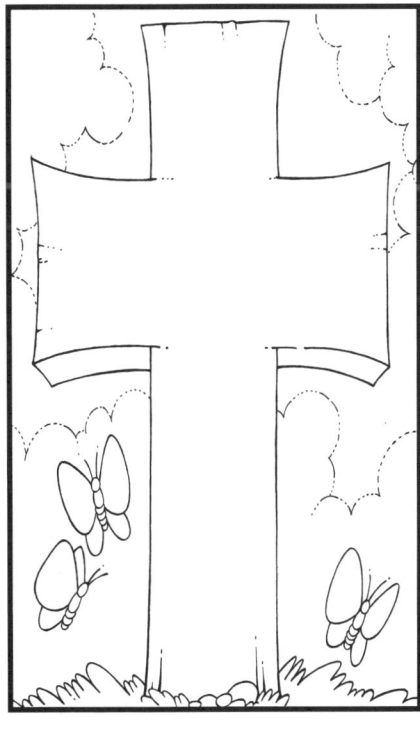

We know that Jesus is God's Son.

PRESCHOOL: LESSON 5   Permission granted to photocopy for local church use. © 2003 Abingdon Press.

Reproducible 5A

Permission granted to photocopy for local church use. © 2003 Abingdon Press.

BibleZone® LIVE

PRESCHOOL: LESSON 5 **Reproducible 5B**
Permission granted to photocopy for local church use. © 2003 Abingdon Press.

Good News In the Garden

Enter the Zone

Bible Verse
Sing happy songs in praise of the LORD.
(Psalm 98:4)

Bible Story
Luke 24:1-12

Our story today celebrates the resurrection of Jesus. On Sunday morning, the women returned to the tomb with the spices that they had prepared. When they got to the tomb, they were very surprised to see the rock rolled away from the opening of the tomb. They went inside and discovered that Jesus was not there. They couldn't understand what had happened.

While they were standing there, they suddenly saw two angels in bright clothing standing next to them. This frightened the women and they fell to the ground. The angels asked the women why they were looking for Jesus there in the tomb. "Don't you remember what Jesus told you?" they asked. Jesus is not here. He is alive. Then the women remembered all that Jesus had told them.

Mary Magdalene, Joanna, Mary the mother of James, and other women were the women who went to the tomb. They hurried back to the disciples and began to tell them excitedly of all that they had seen and heard. The disciples didn't believe them. Can you imagine how frustrating that would have been? Peter ran to the tomb to see if what they had said was true. He wanted to believe. When Peter entered the tomb, he saw only the burial clothes. He returned to the others, trying to understand what had happened.

As we talk about Easter with young children, we celebrate that Jesus is alive. We will use the symbol of the butterfly to remind us of new life. The butterfly reminds us how happy we are that Jesus is alive.

We are happy to know that Jesus is alive.

Scope the Zone

ZONE	TIME	SUPPLIES	ZILLIES
Zoom Into the Zone			
Butterfly Buddies	10 minutes	Reproducible 6A, scissors, crayons or markers, paper plates, glue, envelopes or plastic sandwich bags	none
Decorating the Garden	6 minutes	wooden spring-type clothespins, wiggly eyes, glue, resealable plastic sandwich bags, confetti, pieces of ribbons, chenille stems, masking tape	none
BibleZone			
An Empty Tomb	5 minutes	small meat trays, paper cups, potting soil and/or sod, silk flowers, rocks	none
Hosanna Hop	2 minutes	hosanna hoops	none
Good News	5 minutes	none	none
Bible Verse Buzz	3 minutes	Bible, BZ Bee	none
Praisin' and Singin'	3 minutes	CD player, scarves	CD
LifeZone			
Sharing Easter Joy	5 minutes	Reproducible 6B, paint shallow pans, paper towels	butterfly stamps
Remembering With Friends	5 minutes	CD player	2 plastic baskets and 3 Easter eggs, CD
Butterfly Prayers	2 minutes	none	none

Zillies® are found in the **BibleZone® LIVE FUNspirational® Kit**.

PRESCHOOL: LESSON 6

Zoom Into the Zone

Choose one or more activities to capture the attention of your children.

Supplies:
Reproducible 6A
scissors
crayons or markers
paper plates
glue
envelopes or plastic sandwich bags

Zillies®:
none

Butterfly Buddies

Copy the butterfly puzzle **(Reproducible 6A)** for each child. Have the children cut out the circle. Younger children might need some help. Give each child a paper plate. Have the children color around the edges of the paper plates with crayons and/or markers. Color the picture of the butterfly. Glue the circle in the center of the paper plate. Cut the paper plate in four or five pieces to make a puzzle. Have the children try to put the puzzle back together. Put the puzzle pieces in the envelope or sandwich bag to take home later.

Say: The butterfly reminds us that Jesus is alive. That makes us so happy!

 **We are happy to know that Jesus is alive.**

Supplies:
wooden spring-type clothespins
wiggly eyes
glue
resealable, plastic sandwich bags
confetti, pieces of ribbons, and/or wrapping paper
chenille stems
masking tape

Zillies®:
none

Decorating the Garden

Say: Today we are going to finish our garden where we heard stories about Jesus. We are going to add some butterflies.

Give each child a plastic sandwich bag. Provide a variety of confetti, ribbons, wrapping paper, and so forth for the children to put in their sandwich bags. Close the bag securely. Clip the clothespin in the center of the bag to create the "wings" of the butterfly. On the clothespin, glue on wiggly eyes. Add chenille stem antenna, if you like.

Tape these butterflies to your garden scene to celebrate that Jesus is alive.

Say: We're making a garden to use when we hear stories of Jesus in the garden.

Choose one or more activities to immerse your children in the Bible story.

An Empty Tomb

Give each child a meat tray. Lay the paper cup on its side on the tray. Place potting soil over the top of the cup to create a cave or tomb. Add sod and silk flowers to the top of the potting soil. Place the rock so that it is to the side of the opening.

Say: When the women went to the tomb, they were surprised that Jesus was not there. The angels told them that Jesus was alive. We are so happy that we can celebrate that Jesus is alive.

Hosanna Hop

Use the "Hosanna Hop" to lead your children to the story area. The children can use the hosanna hoops that they made in Lesson 1.

    Hosanna, Hosanna, this is what we say
    (Wave hoops overhead in an arc.)
    Hosanna, Hosanna, we can shout hooray.
    (Jump up in the air, shouting hooray.)
    We love to hear the stories that tell us of the way
    (Cup hand to ear.)
    Jesus taught us how to live and love God everyday.
    (Point up and hug self.)
    Hosanna, Hosanna, let's stomp on down the road.
    (Stomp along.)
    Hosanna, Hosanna, let's ride like Jesus rode.
    (Pretend to ride donkey.)
    Hosanna, Hosanna, let's hop on down the road.
    (Hop along.)
    Hosanna, Hosanna, let's ride like Jesus rode.
    (Pretend to ride donkey.)
    Hosanna, Hosanna, this is what we say
    (Wave hoops over head in an arc.)
    Hosanna, Hosanna, we can shout hooray.
    (Jump up in the air, shouting hooray.)

Supplies:
small meat trays
paper cups
potting soil and/or sod
silk flowers
rocks

Zillies®:
none

Supplies:
hosanna hoops

Zillies®:
none

PRESCHOOL: LESSON 6

Bible Zone Story

Good News

by Beth Parr

Have the children stand in a circle. Have the children echo the story with you.

It was Sunday morning and the sun was shining brightly.
(Pretend to shade eyes.)
The women were walking to the tomb.
(Walk in place.)

They were carrying the spices they had prepared for Jesus.
(Hold spices in hands.)
When they came to the tomb, they were surprised.
(Open mouth and hold hands up in surprise.)

The stone had been rolled back from the entrance to the tomb!
(Pretend to roll stone.)
The women crept inside the tomb.
(Creep.)

They looked around.
(Shade eyes and look around.)
Jesus was not here.
(Shrug shoulders and hold hands, palms up.)

Suddenly two angels stood beside the women.
(Make halo over head.)
The women were so frightened they fell to the ground.
(Kneel down on the ground.)

The angels told the women that Jesus was not there.
(Shake heads no.)
Jesus is alive!
(Lift arms toward sky.)

The women remembered that Jesus had told them what would happen.
(Tap forehead.)
The women ran to tell Jesus' friends.
(Run in place.)

They were so happy.
(Smile and jump up and down.)

Jesus is alive!
(Lift hands to sky.)
Jesus is alive!
(Lift hands to sky.)

Peter ran to the tomb to see if what they said was true.
(Run in place.)
Jesus was not there.
(Hold hands, palms up.)

Jesus is alive!
(Lift hands to sky.)
Jesus is alive!
(Lift hands to sky.)

In With BZ Bee

Bible Verse Buzz

Choose a child to hold the Bible open to Psalm 98:4.

Say: The women and Peter were so happy that Jesus was alive. We are happy to know that Jesus is alive.

Say the Bible verse, "Sing happy songs in praise of the LORD" (Psalm 98:4), for the children. Have the children say the Bible verse after you.

Turn your back to the children or hide your hands underneath a table as you place the BZ Bee puppet (see page 174) on your hand. Turn around or bring the puppet out where the children can see it.

Pretend to make the puppet talk. Change your voice for the puppet:

Bzzz, Bzzz, Bzzz. Hi, everybody! I'm BZ Bee.

Bzzz, Bzzz, Bzzz. I like to taste ears. Do you have ears? Yum, yum, yum. Let me taste.

Go to each child. Encourage, but do not force each child to turn his or her ear toward BZ. Have BZ pretend to taste each child's ears. Have BZ say things like:

**Mmmm. Mmmm. You taste like honey.
Bzzz. Bzzz. You taste like apples.
Yumm. Yumm. You taste like peaches.**

After BZ has tasted each child's ears, **say: Bzzz. Bzzz. Bzzz. I like to taste your ears. They're yummy.** (Rub BZ's stomach.)

Bzzz. Bzzz. Bzzz. I like something else even more than ears. I like the Bible.

Bzzz. Bzzz. Bzzz. You heard a Bible story today. Who went to the tomb to take spices? *(the women)* **What did they find in the tomb?** *(nothing, Jesus was gone)* **What did the angels tell the women?** *(Jesus is not here; Jesus is alive.)* **Who did the women tell?** *(Jesus' friends)*

Bzzz. Bzzz. Bzzz. Jesus' friends were happy to know that Jesus was alive. We are happy that Jesus is alive.

 **We are happy to know that Jesus is alive.**

Bzzz. Bzzz. Bzzz. Let's say the Bible verse together: "Sing happy songs in praise of the LORD" (Psalm 98:4).

Have the children repeat the Bible verse with BZ Bee.

Have BZ Bee say good-bye to the children. Put the puppet away.

Bible

Choose one or more activities to immerse your children in the Bible story.

Supplies:
CD player
scarves

Zillies®:
CD

Praisin' and Singin'

Say: We are so happy that Jesus is alive. Let's sing some songs to celebrate.

Sing the song, "Praisin'" from the **CD (Track 13)**. Give the children scarves to wave as they sing and dance.

Sing "This Special Day" to the tune of "The Wheels on the Bus" **(CD Track 18)**.

This Special Day

On this Easter day let's clap our hands,
(Clap hands.)
Clap our hands, clap our hands.
On this Easter day let's clap our hands,
For Jesus lives.

On this Easter day let's stomp our feet,
(Stomp feet.)
Stomp our feet, stomp our feet.
On this Easter day let's stomp our feet,
For Jesus lives.

On this Easter day let's turn around,
(Turn around.)
Turn around, turn around.
On this Easter day let's turn around,

For Jesus lives.
On this Easter day let's jump for joy,
(Jump for joy.)
Jump for joy, jump for joy.
On this Easter day let's jump for joy,
For Jesus lives.

On this Easter day let's shout, "Hooray!"
(Shout, "Hooray!")
Shout, "Hooray!" Shout, "Hooray!"
On this Easter day let's shout, "Hooray!"
For Jesus lives.

Based on Luke 24:1-10
WORDS: Daphna Flegal
Words © 2001 Abingdon Press

 **We are happy to know that Jesus is alive.**

Life

Choose one or more activities to bring the Bible to life.

Sharing Easter Joy

Copy the Easter card **(Reproducible 6B)** before class. Give each child a copy of the Easter card. Place the paper towels in the shallow pans. Pour a small amount of paint in each pan. Have the children dip their thumbs and fingers in the paint. "Stamp" the paint on the vine growing around the cross to make flowers. Have the children use the butterfly stamps to add butterflies all around the flowers.

Say: These are beautiful Easter cards. Give this to a special friend or member of your family. Tell them that Jesus is alive.

Supplies:
Reproducible 6B
paint
shallow pans
paper towels

Zillies®:
butterfly stamps

Remembering With Friends

Have the children stand in a line. Give the child at one end of the line the yellow basket with the three eggs in it.

Give the purple basket to the child at the other end.

Say: We're going to play a game. We will have to work together with our friends. I am going to play some music while we pass the eggs down the line. _____ (child's' name) will take an egg out of the yellow basket and pass it down the line. When the egg reaches the end, _____ (child's name) will put it in the purple basket. Then we'll all say our Bible verse; "Sing happy songs in praise of the LORD." Then we'll pass another egg and then another. When we have all three eggs in the basket; let's jump for joy, Jesus is alive!

You can play this several times changing the children at the beginning and end of the line.

Supplies:
CD Player

Zillies®:
2 plastic baskets and
   3 Easter eggs
CD

 **We are happy to know that Jesus is alive.**

PRESCHOOL: LESSON 6

Life

Choose one or more activities to bring the Bible to life.

Supplies:
none

Zillies®:
butterfly fans

Butterfly Prayers

Have the children sit down in the worship area. Give each child a fan. If you have a large group, you can do this more than once and let them share the fans.

Say: Today we are celebrating that Jesus is alive. It makes us happy to know that Jesus is alive.

Ask the children to wave their fans in front of them the first three lines of the poem. On the last line, the children will raise their fan and wave it over their head.

> Waving fans can be such fun
> Cool air blows on everyone.
> Wave your fans and let's shout hooray
> Jesus is alive! It's a happy day.

Pray: Dear God, Thank you for your Son Jesus. We are so happy that Jesus is alive. Amen.

Photocopy the HomeZone newsletter to send home to the parents.

 **We are happy to know that Jesus is alive.**

Home Zone For Parents

Bible Verse
Sing happy songs in praise of the LORD.
Psalm 98:4

Bible Story
Luke 24:1-12

Today we are celebrating the good news that Jesus is alive. We have used the butterfly as a symbol of new life. We heard the story of the women who went to the tomb but did not find Jesus there. The angels told them that Jesus was not there because Jesus was alive. The women ran to tell the disciples and others the wonderful news. The disciples did not believe at first. Peter ran quickly to see for himself. What wonderful news! Jesus is alive! We made Easter cards today. Your child may want to share that card with someone special in your family.

Celebrating Easter And New Life

Spend some time together planting bulbs or flowers. Talk about how the beautiful flowers can remind us of the good news that Jesus is alive.

Make a butterfly puppet with craft sticks and cupcake liners. Bunch up the liner to make fluffy wings. Glue this to a craft stick, allowing enough room at the top to draw a face. Glue a second craft stick on top of the first to create the butterfly body with the wings in between. Let your child draw a face on the butterfly. You might make one as well so that you can enjoy "flying around" together.

We are happy to know that Jesus is alive.

PRESCHOOL: LESSON 6   Permission granted to photocopy for local church use. © 2003 Abingdon Press.

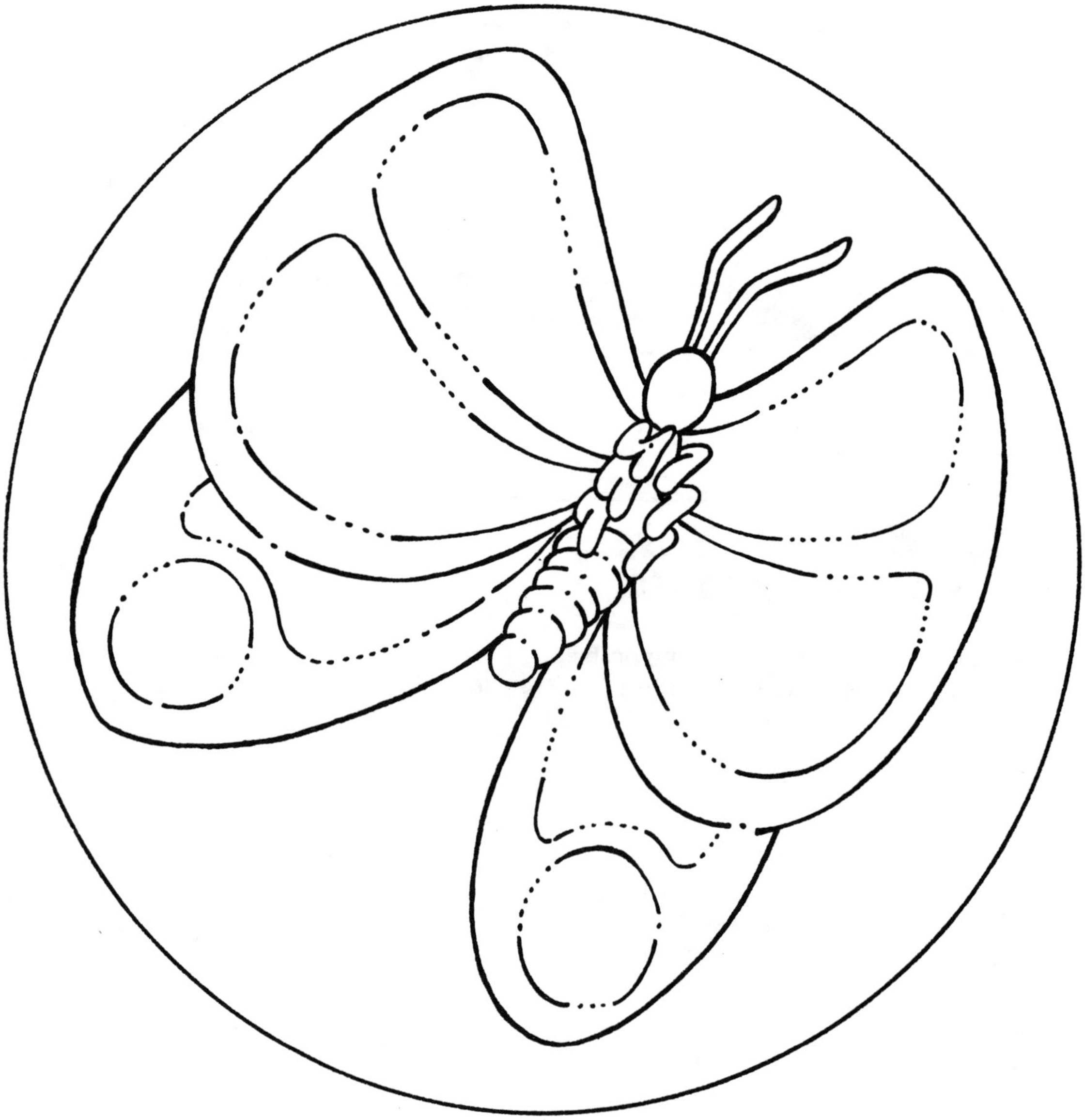

Reproducible 6A

Permission granted to photocopy for local church use. © 2003 Abingdon Press.

BibleZone® LIVE

Preschool: Lesson 6 **Reproducible 6B**
Permission granted to photocopy for local church use. © 2003 Abingdon Press.

No Garden At All

Enter the Zone

Bible Verse
And God saw that it was good.
(Genesis 1:25, NRSV)

Bible Story
Genesis 1:1-13

As we focus on the creation of the world, we are reminded over and over again that God is in control of everything. There was a time when there was no garden, no earth, and no sky. The earth was in a state of swirling chaos. God acted and our world began to take form. With the word of God, light was created, separating night and day. With the Word of God, the sky was created. With the Word of God, dry land and the waters were separated to create earth and seas. Then God spoke and the earth was covered with trees and plants. Through the power of a wonderful God, all of creation came into being.

Not only do we read of the wonder of all that God created, we also understand that God saw that all that had been created was good. God affirmed the fulfillment of God's plan for the universe, by pronouncing creation as good. The word *good* referred not just to beauty, but also to the fact that this creation was pleasing to God.

God's activity on the first three days lays the foundation for the rest of creation. Light and darkness were created first because all of God's creation will be dependent upon light. Light will be necessary for growing plants. Light symbolizes goodness and a banishing of evil. In this creation account, God separates the water from the dry land. Water plays an important role throughout the Old Testament. It is a source of life for the people and for their crops. Water likewise plays a role in the rituals aimed at spiritual cleansing.

Young children observe and celebrate the wonder of creation. We have the great opportunity to experience the awe of young children as they discover God's creation.

We thank God for our beautiful world.

Scope the Zone

ZONE	TIME	SUPPLIES	ZILLIES
Zoom Into the Zone			
Creation Pictures	10 minutes	Reproducible 7A, watercolor markers, water in flat pan or dish, cotton swabs	none
Creating Our World	10 minutes	Transparency 2; overhead projector, bed sheet, bulletin board paper, or dry wall; Reproducible 7C, tempera paint, paintbrushes	none
BibleZone			
A Wonderful World	5 minutes	none	none
Sign a Verse	5 minutes	none	none
No Garden At All	5 minutes	none	none
Bible Verse Buzz	3 minutes	Bible, BZ Bee	none
Sing a Song of Creation	5 minutes	CD player	CD
LifeZone			
Lovely Leaves	5 minutes	leaves, cardboard cut 8 x 11 inches, Styrofoam meat tray, tempera paint, paint roller, thin white paper, glue, paint shirts, newspaper	none
Thank You, God	5 minutes	Reproducible 7B, fabric ribbon, crayons and markers, glue, scissors	none
Creation Prayers	2 minutes	none	inflatable animal ball

Zillies® are found in the **BibleZone® LIVE FUNspirational® Kit.**

Zoom Into the Zone

Choose one or more activities to capture the attention of your children.

Supplies:
Reproducible 7A
watercolor markers
small amount of water in flat pan or dish
cotton swabs

Zillies®:
none

Creation Pictures

Copy the creation picture **(Reproducible 7A)** for each child. Have the children color the picture with watercolor markers. Give each child a cotton swab. Show him or her how to dip the swab in water and "paint" over the picture, creating swirls.

Say: God created the night and the day. God created the sky. God created the earth and the oceans. Everything God created is good.

 **We thank God for our beautiful world.**

Supplies:
Transparency 2
overhead projector
bed sheet, bulletin board paper, or dry wall
Reproducible 7C
tempera paint
paintbrushes

Zillies®:
none

Creating Our World

Say: God created our beautiful world for us to enjoy. We are going to add pieces of our world each week as we hear stories about God's creation. Today we are going to create our creation scene.

Use **Transparency 2** to make a Creation Poster. You will use this poster as the background for the Bible story for the next few weeks. Transfer the design on a bed sheet, bulletin board paper, or a sheet of dry wall. If you would prefer, create your own poster base. Paint the sky on the left side of the poster black to indicate night. Paint the sky on the right side light blue. Color the land brown or green. Color the water blue. Let the children add cotton balls to the sky area on the "day" side to represent clouds. Make a copy of the trees and plants **(Reproducible 7C)** [page 169].

Have the children paint the trees and plants to add to the world. Tape the trees and plants in place. Hang the backdrop in your story area.

Say: God created a wonderful world for us. We'll enjoy learning about all the parts of our world.

BibleZone® LIVE

Choose one or more activities to immerse your children in the Bible story.

A Wonderful World

Supplies:
none

Zillies®:
none

Use "A Wonderful World" to lead your children to the story area.

Look at me and you will see. (*Point to self, circle eyes like glasses.*)
I'm as happy, as happy can be. (*Put fingers at corners of a big smile.*)
God made the world for me and you. ("*Draw*" *a big circle with hands to make the world.*)
Are you happy and smiling too? (*Point away from self; put fingers at corners of smile.*)
Let's stomp, stomp, stomp.
Let's jump, jump, jump.
Let's giggle, giggle, giggle.
Let's hop, hop, hop.
Let's sit right down (*Sit in circle.*)
And now let's stop.
God made the world, everything we see. ("*Draw*" *a big circle with hands to make the world.*)
God made the world for you and me. (*Point out and toward self.*)

Sign a Verse

Supplies:
none

Zillies®:
none

Teach the children the Bible verse with American Sign Language: "And God saw that it was good" (Genesis 1:25, NRSV).

God – Point the index finger of your right hand, with the other fingers curled down. Bring the hand down and open the palm.

Saw – Hold your fingers in a V-shape in front of your eyes. Move the hand forward.

Good – Touch the fingers of your right hand to the lips. Move the hand forward and drop it into the open palm of the left hand.
Repeat several times.

PRESCHOOL: LESSON 7

Bible Zone Story

No Garden At All

by Beth Parr

> Have the children join you in a circle. Have the children join in the response: "Thank you, God, we all gladly say."

Long ago the world was bare
There was no light found anywhere.
The water swirled and swirled around.
It was covering up all of the ground.

God had a plan for you and me.
God created our great world you see.
It's a wonderful place to grow and play.
Thank you, God, we all gladly say.

God made light and called it Day.
"This light is good," God did say.
God took the darkness and called it Night.
This was the first day and all was right.

God had a plan for you and me.
God created our great world you see.
It's a wonderful place to grow and play.
Thank you, God, we all gladly say.

God formed the sky, way up high.
God made the clouds floating by.
The sky was a wonderful, wonderful sight.
This was the second day and all was right.

God had a plan for you and me.
God created our great world you see.
It's a wonderful place to grow and play.
Thank you, God, we all gladly say.

God gathered the water and called it Seas.
God made dry land to grow plants and trees.
"All of this is good," God then did say.
This was the end of the third great day.

God had a plan for you and me.
God created this great world you see.
It's a wonderful place to grow and play.
Thank you, God, we all gladly say.

We thank God for our beautiful world.

In With BZ Bee

Bible Verse Buzz

Choose a child to hold the Bible open to Genesis 1:25, NRSV.

Say: When there was nothing at all, God created a wonderful world. We thank God for our beautiful world.

Say the Bible verse, "And God saw that it was good" (Genesis 1:25, NRSV), for the children. Have the children say the Bible verse after you.

Turn your back to the children or hide your hands underneath a table as you place the BZ Bee puppet (see page 174) on your hand. Turn around or bring the puppet out where the children can see it.

Pretend to make the puppet talk. Change your voice for the puppet:

Bzzz, Bzzz, Bzzz. Hi, everybody! I'm BZ Bee.

Bzzz, Bzzz, Bzzz. I like to taste ears. Do you have ears? Yum, yum, yum. Let me taste.

Go to each child. Encourage, but do not force each child to turn his or her ear toward BZ. Have BZ pretend to taste each child's ears. Have BZ say things like:

**Mmmm. Mmmm. You taste like honey.
Bzzz. Bzzz. You taste like apples.
Yumm. Yumm. You taste like peaches.**

After BZ has tasted each child's ears, **say: Bzzz. Bzzz. Bzzz. I like to taste your ears. They're yummy.** *(Rub BZ's stomach.)*

Bzzz. Bzzz. Bzzz. I like something else even more than ears. I like the Bible.

Bzzz. Bzzz. Bzzz. You heard a Bible story today about God creating the world. What did God make? *(light, night, day, sky, seas, dry land)* **What did God say about the things God created?** *(It was good.)*

Bzzz. Bzzz. Bzzz. God created day and night. God created the sky. God created the seas and earth. What a beautiful world. We thank God for our beautiful world.

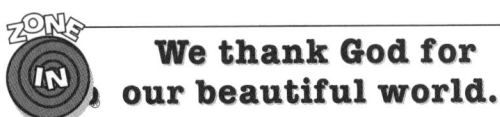
We thank God for our beautiful world.

Bzzz. Bzzz. Bzzz. Let's say the Bible verse together: "And God saw that it was good." (Genesis 1:25, NRSV).

Have the children repeat the Bible verse with BZ Bee.

Have BZ Bee say good-bye to the children. Put the puppet away.

PRESCHOOL: LESSON 7

87

Choose one or more activities to immerse your children in the Bible story.

Supplies:
CD player

Zillies®:
CD

Sing a Song of Creation

Say: After God created the world, God said that it was good. Let's sing a song that reminds us of God's creation.

Sing the refrain of the song "It Is Good" from the **CD (Track 10)**.

It Is Good

It is good, it is good, it is good.
God made it and said, "It's good!"
It is good, it is good, it is good.
God made it and said, "It's good."

WORDS and MUSIC: Keith Brudevold
© 1981 Three Kings Music (BMI).
Used by permission of Keith J. Brudevold, 4400 Taft St.,
Boise, ID 83703

Sign the Bible Verse: "And God saw that it was good" (Genesis 1:25, NRSV).

 **We thank God for our beautiful world.**

Choose one or more activities to bring the Bible to life.

Lovely Leaves

Help children to put on paint shirts or smocks to protect clothing. Cover the table with newspaper. Have the children glue their leaves onto the cardboard. Let them dry for a few minutes. Pour a little paint into the Styrofoam meat tray. Roll the paint roller back and forth in the paint. Roll the roller over the leaves on the cardboard until they are covered with paint. Place the piece of white paper on top of the cardboard. Rub your hand over the paper. Lift the paper. You will have a lovely leaf print.

Say: God created all the plants and trees that we see every day. We have a leaf print to remind us to say thank you to God for our beautiful world.

Thank You, God

Copy the creation cards **(Reproducible 7B)** for each child. Have the children color the pictures with crayons or markers. Cut the cards apart. Glue them to the ribbon so that the ribbon hangs vertically.

Ask the children to tell you about the pictures.

Say: We can thank God for all the wonderful things God placed in our world. What are some of the things in our pictures?

Supplies:
leaves
cardboard cut
   8 x 11 inches
Styrofoam meat tray
   (sanitized with
   bleach solution or
   cleaned in dish-
   washer)
tempera paint
paint roller
thin white paper
glue
paint shirts
newspaper

Zillies®:
none

Supplies:
Reproducible 7B
18-inch length of
   2-inch wide fabric
   ribbon
crayons and markers
glue
scissors

Zillies®:
none

 **We thank God for our beautiful world.**

PRESCHOOL: LESSON 7

Life

Choose one or more activities to bring the Bible to life.

Supplies:
none

Zillies®:
inflatable ball

Creation Prayers

Have the children sit down in a circle in the worship area.

Say: We want to thank God for our beautiful world. I am going to toss the ball to one of you. When you catch the ball, tell us something in our world that God made. Then we will all say, "Thank you, God."

You may need to help the children understand that we are talking about things that God made, not that people made. You may need to offer some suggestions.

Pray:
    Thank you, God, we want to say
    For night and day and earth and seas
    For sky above and plants and trees.
    We thank you, God, today.
    Amen.

Photocopy the HomeZone newsletter to send home to the parents.

 **We thank God for our beautiful world.**

BibleZone® LIVE

Home Zone For Parents

Bible Verse
And God saw that it was good. Genesis 1:25, NRSV

Bible Story
Luke 24:1-12

Today we learned about the first three days of God's creation. We talked about God creating day and night and the sky. We learned that God created the sky, the earth, the ocean, and the plants and trees. We enjoyed sharing the things that we liked most in God's creation. Spend some time outside with your child looking at all the wonder of our world. Collect leaves for a leaf design. When you come in, draw some of the things you saw.

Creation Prayer

Thank you, God, we want to say
For night and day and earth and seas
For sky above and plants and trees.
We thank you, God, today.
Amen.

Leaf Designs

With crayons, help your child color the back of one of the leaves you collected. Place the side you colored down on a piece of paper or cloth. Place another piece of paper on top. Set an iron on warm setting. Iron back and forth over the paper. The color and design from the leaf will show on the bottom sheet of paper. Remove the leaf and enjoy your creation.

We thank God for our beautiful world.

PRESCHOOL: LESSON 7   Permission granted to photocopy for local church use. © 2003 Abingdon Press.

And God saw that it was good.
Genesis 1:25, NRSV

8 BibleZone LIVE

Let There Be Light

Enter the Zone

Bible Verse
And God saw that it was good.
(Genesis 1:25, NRSV)

Bible Story
Genesis 1:14-19

On the fourth day of creation, God created the sun, the moon, and the stars. Day and night were created on the first day. God then added the lights for day and night. God created the sun, the moon, and the stars. Many of the religions in ancient times personified the sun and moon, giving power to these bodies. The sun and moon were worshipped as divine beings. The Genesis story of creation makes it clear that everything is under the power of God. God placed these lights in the sky.

The sun and moon help the people on earth to mark the passage of time. These lights affect the seasons of the year with sunlight lengthening in the summer and becoming very short in the winter. God once again affirms that this part of creation is good. All that God has created is pleasing to God and is intended for the good of the world.

Looking at the creation story with young children helps them to appreciate and talk about the beauty of our world. God had such a magnificent plan for our world. Only God is powerful enough to be able to create a sun so huge to warm the earth and to help plants to grow. Only God could create a moon that changes throughout the month, controlling the tides of the oceans. The children probably will not make the connection between the sun and moon and the seasons of the year. But, they will certainly have lots of questions about the sun and moon and stars. Enjoy learning together. We can always remember that God created the sun, the moon, and the stars.

We thank God for the sun, the moon, and the stars.

Scope the Zone

ZONE	TIME	SUPPLIES	ZILLIES
Zoom Into the Zone			
Star Finger Puppets	10 minutes	Reproducible 8A, glue, glitter, scissors, cotton swabs, stapler	none
Creating Our World	10 minutes	Creation Poster (Transparency 2, Reproducibles 8A, 8B, 5B), tempera paint, paintbrushes, tape	none
BibleZone®			
A Sun of Delight	5 minutes	paper plates, construction paper, sponges, old socks, yarn or rubber band, tempera paint, large craft stick, glue, stapler, aluminum pie tins	none
A Wonderful World	5 minutes	none	none
Sign a Verse	5 minutes	none	none
Let There Be Light	5 minutes	sun and finger puppet stars	none
Bible Verse Buzz	3 minutes	Bible, BZ Bee	none
Creation Song	5 minutes	CD player	CD
LifeZone			
Star Lookers	5 minutes	cardboard tubes, black paper circles, toothpicks, tape or rubber bands, crayons or markers	none
Shiny, Shiny Moon	5 minutes	Reproducible 8B, aluminum foil, paper plates, star stickers, blue markers, tape, scissors, paper punch, yarn	none
Creation Prayers	2 minutes	none	inflatable ball

Zillies® are found in the **BibleZone® LIVE FUNspirational® Kit.**

Preschool: Lesson 8

Zoom Into the Zone

Choose one or more activities to capture the attention of your children.

Supplies:
Reproducible 8A
glue
glitter
scissors
cotton swabs
stapler

Zillies®:
none

Star Finger Puppets

Copy the star finger puppets (**Reproducible 8A**) for each child. Have the children cut out the stars. Younger children may need some help with this. Paint the stars with glue using the cotton swab. Sprinkle with glitter. Let the star dry. Staple the sides together to make a place for fingers. Each child will have four star finger puppets.

Say: God created the stars to shine in the sky at night. They are beautiful for us to see. Let's put our stars on our fingers and make them twinkle in the sky.

We thank God for the sun, the moon, and the stars.

Supplies:
Creation Poster
  (Transparency 2
Reproducibles 8A,
  8B, 5B)
tempera paint
paintbrushes

Zillies®:
none

Creating Our World

Say: God created our beautiful world for us to enjoy. We are going to add pieces of our world each week as we hear stories about God's creation. Today we are going to create our creation scene.

Set up the Creation Poster traced from **Transparency 2** last week in the storytelling area. Point out the night and day, land, sky, and sea.

Make additional copies of the stars (**Reproducible 8A**). Let the children cut them out and paste them in the night sky. Make an additional copy of the moon (**Reproducible 8B**). Paint it and cut it out. Let one of the children add that to the night sky. Make a copy of the sun (**Reproducible 5 B**). Paint it and cut it out. Let one of the children add that to the day sky.

Say: God created a wonderful world for us. We'll enjoy learning about all the parts of our world.

Bible Zone

Choose one or more activities to immerse your children in the Bible story.

A Sun of Delight

Place the paper plates face up. Have the children put glue around the edge of one of the plates. Place construction paper strips on the glue to make the rays of the sun.

Place sponges in the toes of the socks. Close the sock tightly with yarn or a rubber band. Place paint in plates. Have the children turn both of their plates face down. Dip the socks in the paint and color the paper plates.

Allow the plates to dry a little. Staple the plates together, inserting the craft stick to make a handle.

Supplies:
6-inch paper plates,
   2 per child
yellow construction
   paper strips
   (2–inches long)
small sponges
old socks (preferably
   child-size)
yarn or rubber band
yellow tempera paint
large craft stick,
   1 per child
glue
stapler
paper or tin plates
   for paint

Zillies®:
none

A Wonderful World

Look at me and you will see. (*Point to self, circle eyes like glasses.*)
I'm as happy, as happy can be. (*Put fingers at corners of a big smile.*)
God made the world for me and you. (*"Draw" a big circle with hands to make the world.*)
Are you happy and smiling too? (*Point away from self; put fingers at corners of smile.*)
Let's stomp, stomp, stomp.
Let's jump, jump, jump.
Let's giggle, giggle, giggle.
Let's hop, hop, hop.
Let's sit right down (*Sit in circle.*)
And now let's stop.
God made the world, everything we see. (*"Draw" a big circle with hands to make the world.*)
God made the world for you and me. (*Point out and toward self.*)

Use "A Wonderful World" to lead your children to the story area.

Supplies:
none

Zillies®:
none

Sign a Verse

Teach the children the Bible verse with American Sign Language. "And God saw that it was good" (Genesis 1:25, NRSV). (See page 85.)

Repeat several times.

Supplies:
none

Zillies®:
none

Bible Zone Story

Let There Be Light

by Beth Parr

Have the children join you in a circle. Give each child the sun and finger puppet stars they made. Teach the children the motion for moon: Clasp hands overhead, leaning slightly to the right.

Say: *When you hear the word* **sun,** *raise your sun and say "shine, shine." When you hear the word* **stars,** *make your finger puppets move and say "twinkle, twinkle." When you hear the word* **moon,** *do the motion for moon and say "sleep tight."*

On the fourth day of creation, God looked out on the world. God saw the day and the night. God saw the ocean and the land. God saw lots of green trees and plants with fruit growing everywhere.

God decided that the world needed some special lights in the sky. One of these lights would shine during the day and two more lights would shine at night.

God made the sun. *(Shine, shine.)* The sun *(shine, shine)* warmed the earth. The sun *(shine, shine)* appeared in the sky during the day. It was very big and very bright. It added a lot of light to the world. God saw that the sun *(shine, shine)* was very good.

God made the moon. *(Sleep tight.)* The moon *(sleep tight)* appeared in the sky at night. Sometimes the moon *(sleep tight)* was very big. Sometimes the moon *(sleep tight)* looked like it was cut in half. Sometimes it was very small. God saw that the moon *(sleep tight)* was very good.

God added something else to shine at night. God made stars. *(Twinkle, twinkle.)* The stars *(twinkle, twinkle)* looked small because they were so far away. They sparkled in the night. The stars *(twinkle, twinkle)* made pictures in the sky. God saw that the stars *(twinkle, twinkle)* were very good.

What a wonderful day. The world was growing more beautiful. The sun *(shine, shine)* made the world warm and bright. The moon *(sleep tight)* provided light in the night. The stars *(twinkle, twinkle)* made a beautiful night sky. God saw that everything was good.

Thank you, God, for the sun *(shine, shine),* the moon *(sleep tight),* and the stars *(twinkle, twinkle).*

 **We thank God for the sun, the moon, and the stars.**

In With BZ Bee

Bible Verse Buzz

Choose a child to hold the Bible open to Psalm 98:4.

Say: God created a wonderful world when there was nothing at all. God added the sun, the moon, and the stars to make the world even more beautiful.

Say the Bible verse, "And God saw that it was good" (Genesis 1:25, NRSV), for the children. Have the children say the Bible verse after you.

Turn your back to the children or hide your hands underneath a table as you place the BZ Bee puppet (see page 174) on your hand. Turn around or bring the puppet out where the children can see it.

Pretend to make the puppet talk. Change your voice for the puppet:

Bzzz, Bzzz, Bzzz. Hi, everybody! I'm BZ Bee.

Bzzz, Bzzz, Bzzz. I like to taste ears. Do you have ears? Yum, yum, yum. Let me taste.

Go to each child. Encourage, but do not force each child to turn his or her ear toward BZ. Have BZ pretend to taste each child's ears. Have BZ say things like:

Mmmm. Mmmm. You taste like honey.
Bzzz. Bzzz. You taste like apples.
Yumm. Yumm. You taste like peaches.

After BZ has tasted each child's ears, **say:**
Bzzz. Bzzz. Bzzz. I like to taste your ears. They're yummy. *(Rub BZ's stomach.)*
Bzzz. Bzzz. Bzzz. I like something else even more than ears. I like the Bible.

Bzzz. Bzzz. Bzzz. You heard a Bible story today about God adding some great lights to the world. What were these lights? *(sun, moon, and stars)* **What did God say about the things God created?** *(It was good.)*

Bzzz. Bzzz. Bzzz. God created the sun, the moon, and the stars to give light to the world. The sun shines in the day. The moon and stars shine at night. We thank God for our beautiful world.

 **We thank God for the sun, the moon, and the stars.**

Bzzz. Bzzz. Bzzz. Let's say the Bible verse together: "And God saw that it was good" (Genesis 1:25, NRSV).

Have the children repeat the Bible verse with BZ Bee.

Have BZ Bee say good-bye to the children. Put the puppet away.

Choose one or more activities to immerse your children in the Bible story.

Supplies:
CD player

Zillies®:
CD

Creation Song

Say: After God created the world, God said that it was good. Let's sing a song that reminds us of God's creation.

Sing the refrain of the song "It Is Good" from the **CD (Track 10)**.

It Is Good

It is good, it is good, it is good.
God made it and said, "It's good!"
It is good, it is good, it is good.
God made it and said, "It's good."

WORDS and MUSIC: Keith Brudevold
© 1981 Three Kings Music (BMI).
Used by permission of Keith J. Brudevold, 4400 Taft St.,
Boise, ID 83703

Sign the Bible Verse: "And God saw that it was good" (Genesis 1:25, NRSV).

 **We thank God for the sun, the moon, and the stars.**

Choose one or more activities to bring the Bible to life.

Star Lookers

Give each child a cardboard tube. Have the children decorate the outside with crayons or markers. Secure the black circle to one end of each tube with tape or rubber bands. Let the children punch holes in the paper circle with toothpicks. Have the children look at a light through their "star looker." They will see the star picture they created.

Say: God created the stars in the night sky. When we look at them, we can sometimes see pictures. When we look in our "star lookers," we can remember that God created the beautiful, twinkling stars.

Shiny, Shiny Moon

Copy the moon pattern **(Reproducible 8B)** onto heavy paper for each child. Cut out the center of the paper plate for each child. Have the children cut out the moon. Give each child a piece of aluminum foil that will cover the moon. Have the children wrap the moon in the foil. Secure with tape, if needed. Have the children color the outer rim of the plate blue. Add star stickers to make the sky. Punch a hole in the top of the moon. Cut a notch in the top of the paper plate. Thread yarn through the hole and wrap around top of paper plate. Tie a loop for hanging.

Say: We can thank God for the moon. Hang these moons in your room to remind you that God created the moon.

Supplies:
cardboard tube (5–6 inches in length, 1 per child
3-inch black paper circles to cover one end of tube, 1 per child
toothpicks
tape or rubber bands
crayons or markers

Zillies®:
none

Supplies:
Reproducible 8B
aluminum foil
9-inch paper plates, 1 per child
star stickers
blue markers
tape
scissors
paper punch
yarn

Zillies®:
none

 **We thank God for the sun, the moon, and the stars.**

PRESCHOOL: LESSON 8

Choose one or more activities to bring the Bible to life.

Supplies:
none

Zillies®:
inflatable ball

Creation Prayers

Have the children sit down in a circle in the worship area.

Say: We want to thank God for our beautiful world. I am going to toss the ball to one of you. When you catch the ball, tell us something in our world that God made. Then we will all say, "Thank you, God."

You may need to help the children understand that we are talking about things that God made, not that people made. You may need to offer some suggestions.

Pray:
    Thank you, God, we want to say
    For the sun that shines so bright.
    For moon and stars that light the night.
    We thank you God today.
    Amen.

Photocopy the HomeZone newsletter to send home to the parents.

 **We thank God for the sun, the moon, and the stars.**

Home Zone For Parents

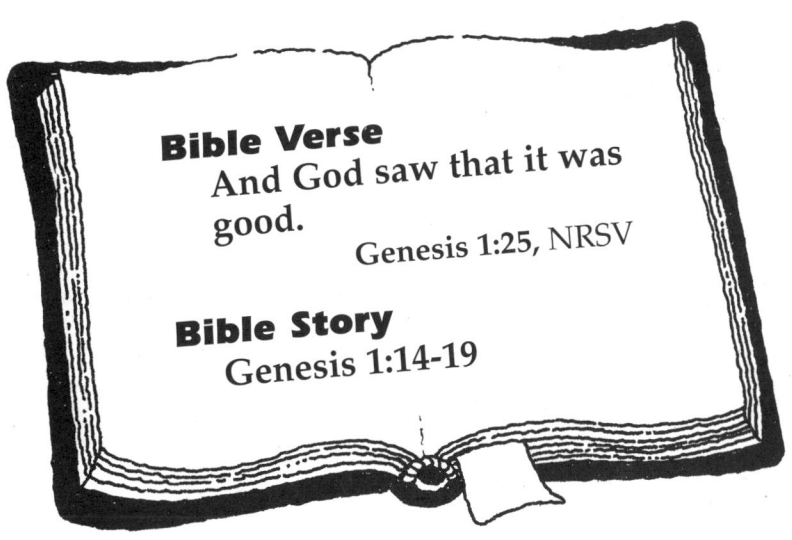

Bible Verse
And God saw that it was good.
Genesis 1:25, NRSV

Bible Story
Genesis 1:14-19

Today our story was about the fourth day of creation. God created the sun to provide warmth and light during the day. God created the moon to add light at night. God added the twinkling stars to brighten the night sky.

Look at pictures of constellations with your child. Go outside at night and try to find some of the constellations in the sky. Talk about how different the moon looks at different times of the month.

Thank God for the sun, moon, and stars. Enjoy being in God's creation.

Star Pictures

On a piece of black or dark blue construction paper, make dots of glue. Sprinkle glitter on the glue to create starbursts.

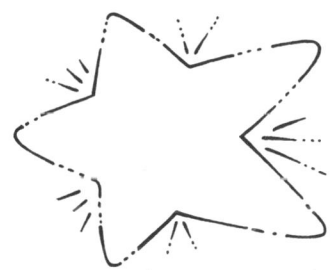

Sun Pictures

Place objects, like blocks, pencils, spoons, and such on a piece of dark construction paper. Put the paper in direct sunlight. Leave the paper outside all day. At the end of the day, take the objects off the paper. What do you see? This shows us how bright the sun shines.

Creation Prayer

Thank you, God, we want to say
For the sun that shines so bright.
For moon and stars that light the night.
Thank you God today.
Amen.

We thank God for the sun, the moon, and the stars.

PRESCHOOL: LESSON 8   Permission granted to photocopy for local church use. © 2003 Abingdon Press.

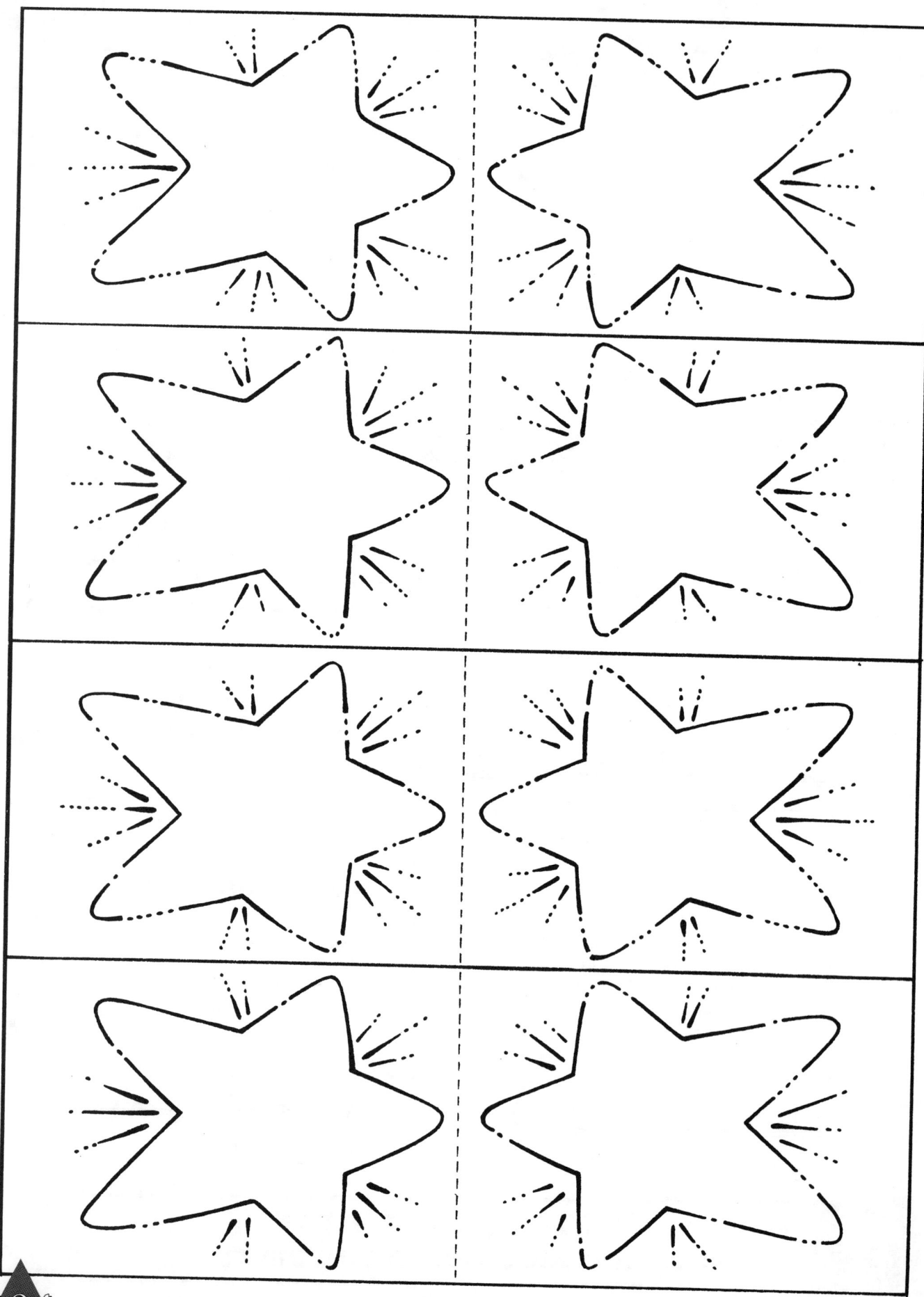

Reproducible 8A

Permission granted to photocopy for local church use. © 2003 Abingdon Press.

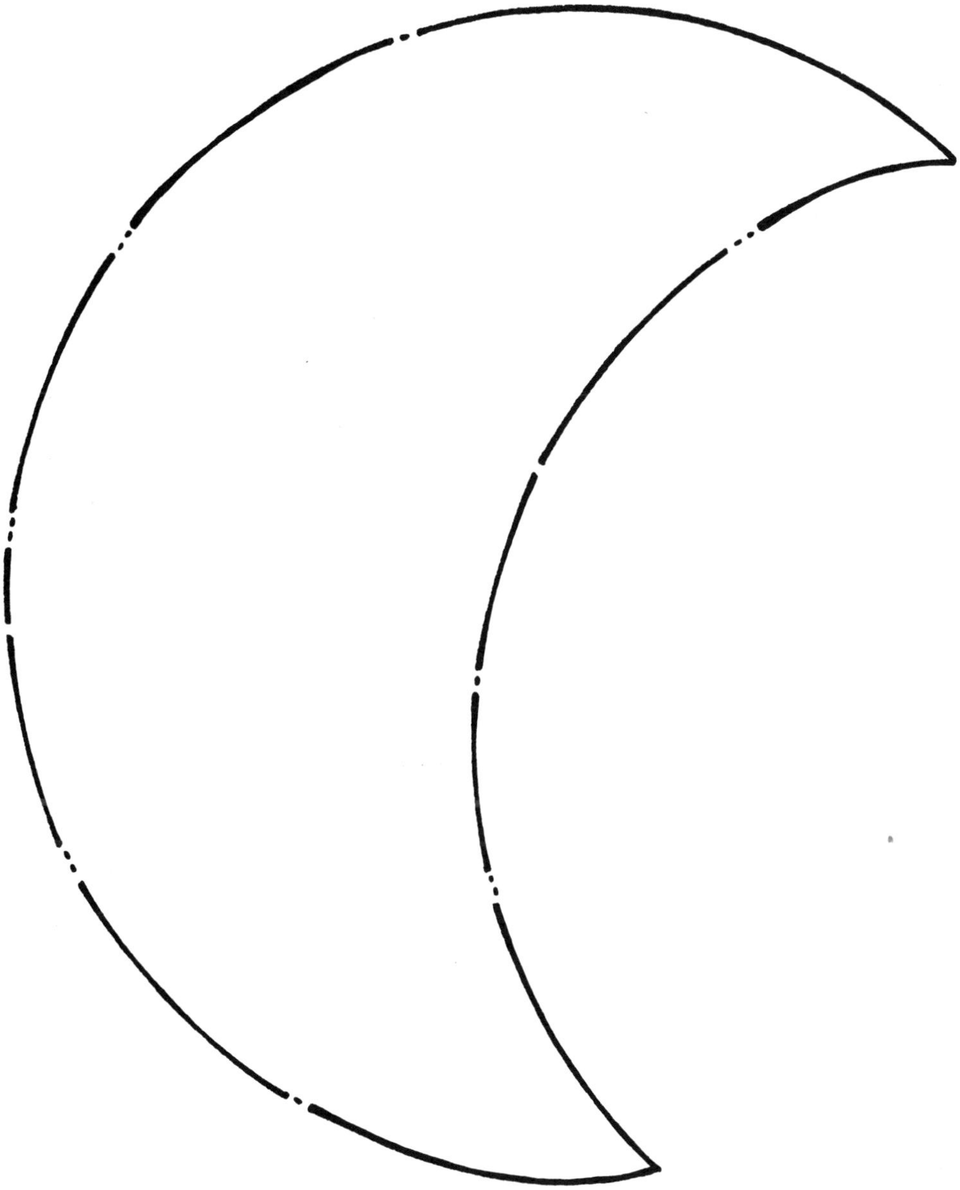

PRESCHOOL: LESSON 8   **Reproducible 8B**

Permission granted to photocopy for local church use. © 2003 Abingdon Press.

Bible Zone LIVE

Filling the Garden

Enter the Zone

Bible Verse
And God saw that it was good.
(Genesis 1:25, NRSV)

Bible Story
Genesis 1:9-13, 20-25

What a magnificent garden God had created! There were lush trees bearing delicious fruit. There were plants of every kind with seeds of all descriptions. What a wonderful place it would be to live. God began to fill the garden with many different kinds of animals. These animals would live and grow in the beauty of the garden. The plants would provide food for them.

God created fish to fill the oceans. There were large fish, colorful fish, and really strange looking fish. Think of all the different kinds of fish there are. God made such interesting creatures to live in the waters of our world.

God created birds to fly above the earth in the sky. God gave them beautiful songs to sing. God gave them wings to soar above the earth. Many different kinds of birds live all over our world.

When God created the animals, God created wild animals, like lions and bears, and domestic animals, like cows and pigs. God created insects, even those pesky mosquitoes. God created reptiles, such as turtles, snakes, and alligators.

God planned for the trees and plants. God planned for the fish and the birds. God planned for all the different types of animals that live in this world. Once again God looked at all of creation and saw that it was good. God created the living creatures of the world and loved each one of them.

Young children enjoy the opportunity to look at many different types of animals, fish and birds. Guide them to see that God created and cares for all of these creatures. We are so blessed that God has provided such a wonderful world in which we can live. There are some animals that we like and some that we don't like. God loved all of creation, even the mosquitoes.

We thank God for the fish, the birds, and the animals.

Scope the Zone

ZONE	TIME	SUPPLIES	ZILLIES®
Zoom Into the Zone			
Animal Garden	10 minutes	Reproducible 9A, markers or crayons, green art tissue, glue	animal stickers
Creating Our World	10 minutes	Creation Poster (Transparency 2), Reproducible 9C, fake fur, tape, paint, paintbrushes	inflatable jumbo monkey
All God's Creatures	5 minutes	Reproducible 9B, crayons or markers, scissors, plastic sandwich bags	none
BibleZone®			
Birds of a Feather	5 minutes	paper plates, tempera paint, construction paper, feathers, scissors, tape, paper punch, yarn	none
Animal Friends Hop	3 minutes	none	none
Filling the Garden	5 minutes	none	none
Bible Verse Buzz	3 minutes	Bible, BZ Bee	CD
A Wonderful World	3 minutes	CD player	none
Sign a Verse	3 minutes	none	CD
LifeZone			
Fishy Friends	10 minutes	shoe boxes, blue paint, glitter, fish sticker, sponges, plates, plastic wrap, tape, glue	none
Animal Toss	3 minutes	clothesbasket	zoo animal porcupine balls
Creation Prayers	2 minutes	none	zoo animal finger puppets

Ⓞ Zillies® are found in the **BibleZone® LIVE FUNspirational® Kit.**

PRESCHOOL: LESSON 9

Zoom Into the Zone

Choose one or more activities to capture the attention of your children.

Supplies:
Reproducible 9A
markers or crayons
green tissue paper
glue

Zillies®:
animal stickers

Animal Garden

Copy the garden picture (**Reproducible 9A**) for each child. Have the children color the picture. Add green tissue paper to the trees and plants. Give each child stickers to add to their garden.

Say: God created all kinds of animals to live in the beautiful garden. We are adding animals to our garden too. We are so happy that God created animals to live on the earth with us.

 **We thank God for the fish, the birds, and the animals.**

Supplies:
Creation Poster
  (Transparency 2)
Reproducible 9C
fake fur
tape
tempera paint

Zillies®:
inflatable jumbo
  monkey

Creating Our World

Say: God created our beautiful world for us to enjoy. We are going to add some pieces to the picture of our world.

Set up the Creation Poster (**Transparency 2**) in the storytelling area. Make a copy of the animal pictures (**Reproducible 9C**) [page 173]. Cut out these pictures. Let the children paint the pictures of the animals. They may glue fake fur on some of the animals. Tape the animals to the creation scene. Inflate and add the **monkey** to the story area.

Say: God created a wonderful world for us. Today we're adding animals. We are also going to add some birds and fish. We can thank God for our wonderful world and all the animals, birds, and fish.

Supplies:
Reproducible 9B
crayons or markers
scissors
plastic sandwich
  bags

Zillies®:
none

All God's Creatures

Copy the memory game cards (**Reproducible 9B**) for each child. Make one extra copy for a class game. Have the children color the pictures. Cut the pictures apart and place them in the plastic sandwich bags.

Using the class set of cards, turn all cards face down on the table. Let the children take turns turning over two cards to see if they find a match. When a child finds a match, **say:** "Thank you God for _____ (name of animal).

Say: You have a set of cards to take home so that you can match the creatures God made.

BibleZone® LIVE

Bible

Choose one or more activities to immerse your children in the Bible story.

Birds of a Feather

Fold the paper plates for the children. Cut along the inside circle of the plate. Stop cutting 1 to 1½ inch before you reach the fold. These flaps will make the wings of the bird. Let the children help you tape the edges of the paper plate together. Have the children paint their birds by dipping feathers in the paint. Cut out a triangle from the construction paper and at one end to make a beak for the bird. Have the children draw an eye on each side of the bird. Punch a hole in the middle near the fold. Thread the yarn through the hole and tie with a knot. Bend the wing flaps out so the bird can take flight.

Fly the birds around the room to the story area. Hang them on the creation story scene or from the ceiling.

Say: God created many different kinds of birds for our world.

Supplies:
6-inch paper plates, 1 per child
tempera paint
construction paper scraps
scissors
tape
paper punch
yarn (12-inch pieces)
feathers

Zillies®:
none

Zoo Animal Friends

Say: God created lots of creatures to live in the garden. We have our friends, *(name the two finger puppets)*, hopping by to visit us. We're going to play a little game with our animal friends.

Divide the children into two groups. Sit them in lines across from each other. Call one child's name. That child will hop one of the animals across to the other line. They will say the name of an animal. Call a child's name from the other line. They will hop their animal to the other line and name an animal. Continue until every child has had a chance. You may want to make a list of all the animals they name.

Say: Our animal friends helped us to remember that God created many different animals that live in our world.

Supplies:
none

Zillies®:
zoo animal finger puppets

 **We thank God for the fish, the birds, and the animals.**

PRESCHOOL: LESSON 9

Bible Zone Story

Filling the Garden

by Beth Parr

Have the children join you in an echo pantomime.

God created a garden filled with trees
(Hold arms up like branches of a tree.)
The branches of the trees blew in the breeze.
(Sway back and forth, waving "branches.")
There were green plants growing everywhere.
(Point all around you.)
There were seeds from the plants blowing here and there.
(Pretend to blow seeds from your hand.)

God made cows to live in this land
(Moo, moo.)
God made pigs that like rolling around
(Oink, oink.)
God made tigers and lions that roar.
(Roar.)
God made birds in the sky to soar.
(Hold arms out and flap wings.)

God made alligators with great big mouths
(Make alligator mouth with arms.)
God made eagles that soar in the clouds.
(Hold arms out to the side and fly.)
God made dolphins that live in the sea.
(Put hands together to swim back and forth like a fish.)
God make giraffes that eat the high leaves.
(Extend neck and pretend to eat.)

God made elephants with trunks so long.
(Hold arm in front of face like an elephant trunk.)
God made robins that sing a sweet song.
(Chirp, chirp.)

What a wonderful world God made for us all.
(Make world with arms.)
God made animals that are big and small.
(Hold hand up high for big and cup hands for small.)

God made mosquitoes and bees that buzz.
(Buzz, buzz.)
God made caterpillars all covered with fuzz.
(Make finger caterpillar to climb up arm.)
All of the creatures that live in this land,
(Make world with arms; spread arms with palms up.)
Yes, everything was part of God's plan.
(Nod head yes.)

God looked out on all that was made.
(Hold hand above eyes and look around.)
"It is good" was what God had to say.
We thank you, God, for your wonderful plan
(Fold hands in prayer.)
For birds, animals, and fish that live in our land.

We thank God for the fish, the birds, and the animals.

In With BZ Bee

Bible Verse Buzz

Choose a child to hold the Bible open to Genesis 1:25, NRSV.

Say: God created a wonderful garden with plants and trees. God added animals, birds, and fish. What a wonderful world God created.

Say the Bible verse, "And God saw that it was good" (Genesis 1:25, NRSV), for the children. Have the children say the Bible verse after you.

Turn your back to the children or hide your hands underneath a table as you place the BZ Bee puppet (see page 174) on your hand. Turn around or bring the puppet out where the children can see it.

Pretend to make the puppet talk. Change your voice for the puppet:

Bzzz, Bzzz, Bzzz. Hi, everybody! I'm BZ Bee.

Bzzz, Bzzz, Bzzz. I like to taste ears. Do you have ears? Yum, yum, yum. Let me taste.

Go to each child. Encourage, but do not force each child to turn his or her ear toward BZ. Have BZ pretend to taste each child's ears. Have BZ say things like:

Mmmm. Mmmm. You taste like honey.
Bzzz. Bzzz. You taste like apples.
Yumm. Yumm. You taste like peaches.

After BZ has tasted each child's ears, **say: Bzzz. Bzzz. Bzzz. I like to taste your ears. They're yummy.** *(Rub BZ's stomach.)*

Bzzz. Bzzz. Bzzz. I like something else even more than ears. I like the Bible.

Bzzz. Bzzz. Bzzz. You heard a Bible story today about God adding some creatures to live in the land? What were some of the animals God made? *(cow, pig, elephant, and so on)* **What else did God make?** *(birds and fish)* **What did God say after making all of these creatures?** *(It was good.)*

Bzzz. Bzzz. Bzzz. God created the animals, birds, and fish. We thank God for our beautiful world.

 **We thank God for the fish, the birds, and the animals.**

Bzzz. Bzzz. Bzzz. Let's say the Bible verse together: "And God saw that it was good." (Genesis 1:25, NRSV)

Have the children repeat the Bible verse with BZ Bee.

Have BZ Bee say good-bye to the children. Put the puppet away.

Choose one or more activities to immerse your children in the Bible story.

Supplies:
CD player

Zillies®:
CD

A Wonderful World

Use "A Wonderful World" to lead your children to the story area.

Look at me and you will see. (*Point to self, circle eyes like glasses.*)
I'm as happy, as happy can be. (*Put fingers at corners of a big smile.*)
God made the world for me and you. ("*Draw" a big circle with hands to make the world.*)
Are you happy and smiling too? (*Point away from self; put fingers at corners of smile.*)
Let's stomp, stomp, stomp.
Let's jump, jump, jump.
Let's giggle, giggle, giggle.
Let's hop, hop, hop.
Let's sit right down (*Sit in circle.*)
And now let's stop.
God made the world, everything we see. ("*Draw" a big circle with hands to make the world.*)
God made the world for you and me. (*Point out and toward self.*)

Supplies:
none

Zillies®:
none

Sign a Verse

Sign the Bible verse with the children in American Sign Language: "And God saw that it was good" (Genesis 1:25, NRSV). (See page 85)

Choose one or more activities to bring the Bible to life.

Fishy Friends

Give each child a shoebox. Have them sponge paint the inside of the shoebox with the blue paint to create the ocean. Let it dry a little. Add fish stickers or glue pictures of fish to the ocean. If you like, glue seashells to box. Cover the front of the box with plastic wrap. Secure it with tape. Let the children enjoy looking at "their fish."

Say: God created the fish that live in water all around our world. When we look at our fish, we can remember that God created all kinds of fish for our world.

Supplies:
shoe box, 1 per child
blue paint with glitter
fish stickers
sponges
plates for paint
plastic wrap
tape
glue
seashells (optional)

Zillies®:
none

Animal Toss

Say: We're going to play a game with our animal friends. You will have a chance to toss the animal in the basket. When you toss the animal, call out the name of the animal. We will all say our Bible verse, "And God saw that it was good" (Genesis 1:25, NRSV).

Enjoy playing till every child has had a turn.

Say: We can thank God for all the animals that live in our world.

Supplies:
clothesbasket

Zillies®:
zoo animal porcupine balls

We thank God for the fish, the birds, and the animals.

PRESCHOOL: LESSON 9

Choose one or more activities to bring the Bible to life.

Supplies:
none

Zillies®:
2 animal finger puppets

Creation Prayers

Have the children sit down in a circle in the worship area.

Say: We have our friends, Monte and Tigger, with us today for our prayers.

Let Monte say: Hello, boys and girls, we heard about all the creatures God made for the world. Can you name some of the animals? *(Let the children answer.)* **That's great! You know about lots of animals. Tigger, did you hear that?**

Let Tigger say: I sure did. Can you tell me what else God made? *(birds and fish—children may include these with the animals)* **We need to thank God. Can you say "Thank you, God" with me?** *(Let children respond.)*

Say: We are going to pray now. I'm going to say a line and then you say "Thank you, God."

Pray:
    For animals that walk upon the land,
    Thank you, God.
    For birds that fly as high as they can,
    Thank you, God.
    For fish that swim in the deep blue sea.
    Thank you, God.
    For this wonderful world you made for me.
    Thank you, God.
    Amen.

Photocopy the HomeZone newsletter to send home to the parents.

Home Zone For Parents

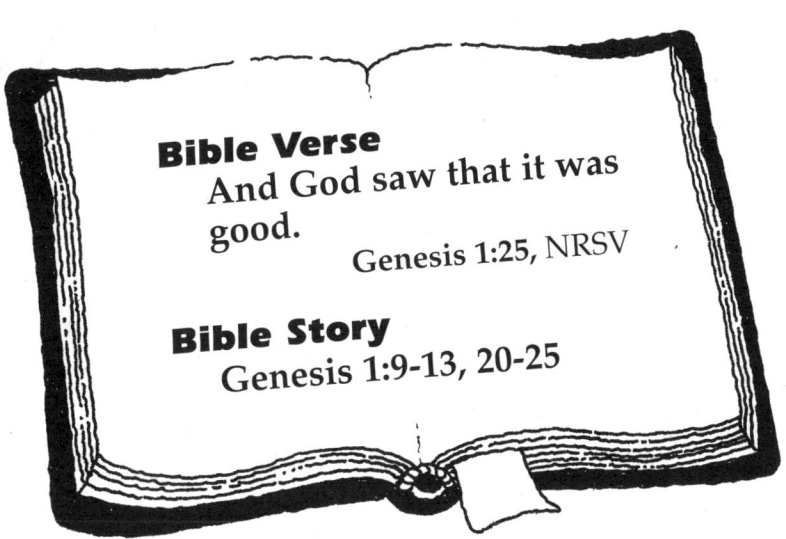

Bible Verse
And God saw that it was good.
Genesis 1:25, NRSV

Bible Story
Genesis 1:9-13, 20-25

Our story today focused on all the wonderful creatures that God created for our world. We thanked God for animals, for birds, and for fish. God had created a beautiful green garden and a deep blue sea. God had created the sky. Now God made living creatures to inhabit these places: the animals, the birds, and the fish.

Visit a zoo, pet store, or aquarium. If this isn't possible, look at books with your child that show the different kinds of animals, birds, and fish. Ask your child about their favorite animal. Enjoy making animal noises. Thank God for the fish, birds, and animals. Enjoy spotting new creatures in God's creation.

Let's Be Elephants

Cut a paper plate in half. Each half will be used to make elephant ears. Color the ears gray. Cut a small slit in the corner of each ear. Use a strip of construction paper to make a headband for you and for your child. Slip the headband into the ears. Tape the ears so they won't fall off. Take another piece of construction paper. Roll the paper to make a tube. Tape it together. Tape the roll to the headband to make the elephant's trunk. Enjoy being elephants that stomp along swinging their trunks. Thank God for elephants.

Creation Prayer

Thank you, God,
we want to say
For animals that walk upon the land,
For birds that fly
as high as they can,
For fish that swim in the deep blue sea.
For this wonderful world you made for me.
Thank you God today.
Amen.

We thank God for the fish, the birds, and the animals.

Preschool: Lesson 9 — **Reproducible 9B**

Tending The Garden

Enter the Zone

Bible Verse
And God saw that it was good.
(Genesis 1:25, NRSV)

Bible Story
Genesis 1:26-31

God prepared a wonderful garden. The garden was filled with plants and trees bearing fruit to provide food. God filled the garden with animals and birds. God filled the waters with fish. God saw that all of this creation was good. On the sixth day, God added the creation of humankind.

These people were made in God's image. What did this mean? God created humans as representatives of God. God gave human beings the ability to think, to feel, and to make decisions. These people were created male and female.

After creating human beings, God gave them a responsibility. God told them that they would have power over the fish and the birds. They would have power over all living things. God gave human beings this power not for selfish pursuits. God gave this power so that the people would take care of creation. It was their responsibility to make sure that everything proceeded according to God's plan.

God told the human beings that plants were provided to give food to them and to all the living creatures of the earth. God was telling these human creations that they were being provided with everything they needed. Their response in gratitude and responsibility was to take care of God's creation.

After creating human beings in God's likeness, God looked out on all creation. God saw everything. God did not see that it was good; God saw that it was very good. God had created a world filled with many, special creations. After entrusting this creation to the humans that had just been created, God rested and blessed all that had been done.

God made each one of us a unique person. Every child that is in your class is special. Each child has special abilities and challenges. God created us and loved us. Help the children in your class to recognize that God creates us all and we are all special. We can begin early to teach acceptance of people who are different from us. God created people and God said it was very good.

We thank God for people.

Scope the

ZONE	TIME	SUPPLIES	ⓞ ZILLIES®
Zoom Into the Zone			
Look at Me: I'm a Creation	10 minutes	Reproducible 10A, construction paper, fabric scraps, trim, mirrors, markers or crayons, yarn, glue, scissors	none
Creation Cube Game	5 minutes	Transparency 3, overhead projector, Reproducible 10B, buttons or squares of paper	none
People Print Pictures	5 minutes	drawing paper, ink pad, pens, crayons or markers	none
BibleZone®			
Making People	10 minutes	sand clay, newspapers, cookie sheet	CD
Animal Friends	5 minutes	none	zoo animal finger puppets
Tending the Garden	5 minutes	none	none
Bible Verse Buzz	5 minutes	Bible, BZ Bee	none
A Wonderful World	5 minutes	none	none
Sign a Verse	5 minutes	none	none
Sing a Creation Song	5 minutes	CD player	CD
LifeZone			
People Puppets	10 minutes	roll of butcher paper, markers or crayons, rubber bands, scissors, CD Player	CD
Animal Toss	3 minutes	clothesbasket	zoo animal porcupine balls
Creation Prayers	2 minutes	none	zoo animal finger puppets

ⓞ Zillies® are found in the **BibleZone® LIVE FUNspirational® Kit.**

PRESCHOOL: LESSON 10

Zoom Into the Zone

Choose one or more activities to capture the attention of your children.

Supplies:
Reproducible 10A
construction paper
fabric scraps
buttons, ribbons
mirrors
markers or crayons
yarn
glue
scissors

Zillies®:
none

Look At Me: I'm a Creation

Copy the person cutout **(Reproducible 10A)** for each child. Have the children cut out the person. You may need to help the younger children. Have the children glue the figure onto the construction paper. Ask the children to look in the mirrors.

Say: God created lots of things. One of things God created was you and me. After you have looked at yourself in the mirror, make your person figure on the construction paper look like you.

Post the finished pictures around your room.

We thank God for people.

Supplies:
Transparency 3
overhead projector
Reproducible 10B
buttons or squares of paper for markers

Zillies®:
none

Creation Cube Game

Make a copy of the game cube **(Transparency 3)** on poster paper. Cut out and make into a cube. This is great fun when the cube is large. Make copies of the game card **(Reproducible 10B)** for each child. Pick a child to roll the cube. When it lands, ask that child to call out the part of creation they see on the cube. All the children should then mark their card with the buttons or squares of paper. Ask another child to roll the cube. Continue until the cards are filled up. Everyone then stands up and says: "I am special. God made me."

Supplies:
drawing paper (cut into 4 x 6 inch pieces)
inkpad
pens
crayons or markers

Zillies®:
none

People Print Pictures

Say: God made each one of us very special. We all have fingerprints but our fingerprints are different. Use your fingerprints to make some people on your paper.

You may need to show the children how to draw a face or hair or clothes on their fingerprint.

BibleZone® LIVE

Choose one or more activities to immerse your children in the Bible story.

Making People

Make sand clay or another favorite recipe ahead of time.
Sand Clay
1 cup of play sand
½ cup of cornstarch
½ cup of boiling water
double boiler

Mix the play sand and the cornstarch in the top pot of the double boiler. Pour the boiling water into the sand and cornstarch. Stir it until it is mixed very well. Cook it for a few minutes until it thickens. If it gets too thick, you can add more water. Cool the sand clay slightly before giving it to the children.

Have the children mold the sand clay into people. Place the sand people on a cookie sheet. Cook in a 275-degree oven until the models are dry.

Say: God created each one of us. We have made some people to remind us that God loves each one of us. We are special because God made us.

Supplies:
sand clay ingredients
newspapers
cookie sheet

Zillies®:
CD

Zoo Animal Friends

Say: God created people to live in the garden and take care of the rest of God's creation. We have our friends,(name of the two animals)**, hopping by to visit us. We're going to play a little game with our animal friends.**

Divide the children into two groups. Sit them in lines across from each other. Call one child's name. That child will hop one of the animals across to the other line. When they get to the other side, they will name something that God created. Call a child's name from the other line. They will hop their animal to the other line and name another creation. Continue until every child has had a chance.

Say: Our animal friends helped us to remember that God created a wonderful world with lots of animals, birds, fish, and us.

Supplies:
none

Zillies®:
zoo animal finger puppets

Preschool: Lesson 10

Bible Story

Tending the Garden

by Beth Parr

Have the children join you in a circle. Teach the children the refrain: "Wow, what a world. Thank you, God."

God made the world filled with lots of good things. God made night and day. God made the sky over our heads. God made land so that there would be a dry place for animals to live.
Wow, what a world.
Thank you, God.

God made trees with delicious fruit on them. There were plants everywhere that the animals could eat. There were seeds on the plants so that more plants could grow.
Wow, what a world.
Thank you, God.

There was a bright sun in the sky that warmed the earth. There was a moon and stars that shined in the night. The sun, moon, and stars would give light to the world.
Wow, what a world.
Thank you, God.

God made birds that fly in the sky. God made the ocean and all the fish that live there. The waters on the earth were soon full of fish. There were so many different kinds of birds flying everywhere.
Wow, what a world.
Thank you, God.

God then made animals to live on the dry land. There were lots of different animals. There were horses and dogs. There were tigers and giraffes. There were turtles and frogs. God made elephants and kangaroos.
Wow, what a world.
Thank you, God.

God wasn't finished yet. It was true that the garden was beautiful. It was true that God had created a wonderful world. God needed someone to help take care of creation. God needed someone really special.
Wow, what a world.
Thank you, God.

God decided to make people. These people would be male and female, boys and girls. God made these people so that they could think and plan. They could take care of God's creation.
Wow, what a world.
Thank you, God.

On the sixth day of creation, God made people. "Take care of everything you see," God said. God was very pleased. In fact, God said that everything was very good.
Wow, what a world.
Thank you, God.

In With BZ Bee

Bible Verse Buzz

Choose a child to hold the Bible open to Genesis 1:25, NRSV.

Say: God created a wonderful world but God wasn't finished yet. God wanted to make some people who would help to take care of creation.

Say the Bible verse, "And God saw that it was good" Genesis 1:25, NRSV), for the children. Have the children say the Bible verse after you.

Turn your back to the children or hide your hands underneath a table as you place the BZ Bee puppet (see page 174) on your hand. Turn around or bring the puppet out where the children can see it.

Pretend to make the puppet talk. Change your voice for the puppet:

Bzzz, Bzzz, Bzzz. Hi, everybody! I'm BZ Bee.

Bzzz, Bzzz, Bzzz. I like to taste ears. Do you have ears? Yum, yum, yum. Let me taste.

Go to each child. Encourage, but do not force each child to turn his or her ear toward BZ. Have BZ pretend to taste each child's ears. Have BZ say things like:

Mmmm. Mmmm. You taste like honey.
Bzzz. Bzzz. You taste like apples.
Yumm. Yumm. You taste like peaches.

After BZ has tasted each child's ears, **say: Bzzz. Bzzz. Bzzz. I like to taste your ears. They're yummy.** (Rub BZ's stomach.)

Bzzz. Bzzz. Bzzz. I like something else even more than ears. I like the Bible.

Bzzz. Bzzz. Bzzz. You heard a Bible story today about God making a special creation. What was that? (people) **What did God tell the people to do?** (take care of creation) **What did God say after making everything?** (It was very good.)

Bzzz. Bzzz. Bzzz. God created people, just like you and me. God wants us to help to take care of this world God has given us.

 **We thank God for people.**

Bzzz. Bzzz. Bzzz. Let's say the Bible verse together: "And God saw that it was good" (Genesis 1:25, NRSV).

Have the children repeat the Bible verse with BZ Bee.

Have BZ Bee say good-bye to the children. Put the puppet away.

PRESCHOOL: LESSON 10

Bible

Choose one or more activities to immerse your children in the Bible story.

Supplies:
none

Zillies®:
none

Supplies:
none

Zillies®:
none

Supplies:
CD player

Zillies®:
CD

A Wonderful World

Use "A Wonderful World" to lead your children to the story area. (See Lesson 7, page 85).

Sign a Verse

Sign the Bible verse with the children in American Sign Language. "And God saw that it was good" (Genesis 1:25, NRSV). (See Lesson 7, page 85.)

Sing a Creation Song

Say: After God created the world; God said that it was good. Let's sing a song about the people that God created.

Sing the song, "People Parade" to the tune of "The Wheels on the Bus" from the **CD (Track 18)**.

Our God made people everywhere,
Everywhere, everywhere.
Our God make people everywhere,
And saw that it was good.

Our God made people run, run, run!
Run, run, run! Run, run, run!
Our God make people run, run, run!
And saw that it was good.

Our God made people hop, hop, hop!
Hop, hop, hop! Hop, hop, hop!
Our God made people hop, hop, hop!
And saw that it was good.

Our God made people, tip, tip, toe!
Tip, tip, toe! Tip, tip, toe!
Our God made people, tip, tip, toe!
And saw that it was good.

Our God made people shake, shake, shake!
Shake, shake, shake! Shake, shake, shake!
Our Godh made people shake, shake, shake!
And saw that it was good.

Our God made people everywhere,
Everywhere, everywhere.
Our God made people everywhere.
And saw that it was good.

Based on Genesis 1:26-27
WORDS: Daphna Flegal
Words © 2000 Cokesbury

Choose one or more activities to bring the Bible to life.

People Puppets

Let each child lay down on a length of butcher paper. Trace around their body. Be sure they have their arms stretched out so they can hold the hands of their person. Let them cut the figure out. The younger children may need help. Let the children decorate the person with markers and crayons. When the children finish creating their person, help them to rubber band the feet of the paper person to their shoes. Have the children hold the hands of their person and dance to the music on the **CD**.

Say: God created people. People are all very different, but we are all God's creation. We can enjoy dancing with our friends and remembering that God loves us.

You may want to ask if their friend has a name.

Supplies:
roll of butcher paper
markers or crayons
rubber bands
scissors
CD Player

Zillies®:
CD

Animal Toss

Say: We're going to play a game with our animal friends. You will have a chance to toss the animal in the basket. When you toss the animal, call out the name of one of your friends. That person will go get the animal out of the basket. We will all say our Bible verse, "And God saw that it was good" (Genesis 1:25, NRSV).

Enjoy playing till every child has had a turn.

Say: We can thank God for making people.

Supplies:
clothesbasket

Zillies®:
zoo animal porcupine balls

 **We thank God for people.**

PRESCHOOL: LESSON 10

Life Zone

Choose one or more activities to bring the Bible to life.

Supplies:
none

Zillies®:
2 animal finger puppets

Creation Prayers

Have the children sit down in a circle in the worship area.

Say: We have our animal friends with us today for our prayers.

Let one of the animals say: **Hello, boys and girls, we heard about all the special creatures God made to take care of the world. What were those creatures called?** *(people)* **Oh, that's right! People just like you. Look at all these people.**

Let the other animal say: **Wow, look at them. They all look different. Some have long hair and some have short hair. Some are boys and some are girls. Can you pray with me?**

Pray:
    Thank you, God, we want to say
    For making us to laugh and play.
    For people living in God's way.
    We thank you, God, today.
    Amen.

Photocopy the HomeZone newsletter to send home to the parents.

BibleZone® LIVE

Home Zone For Parents

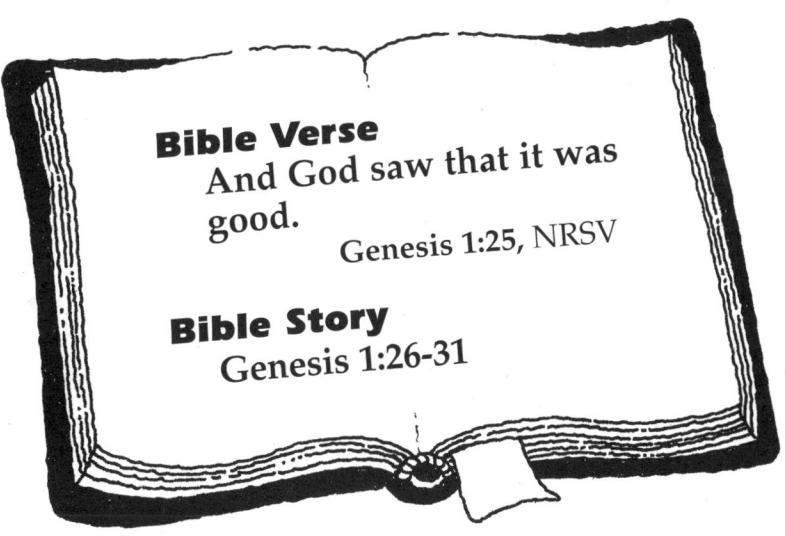

Bible Verse
And God saw that it was good.
Genesis 1:25, NRSV

Bible Story
Genesis 1:26-31

God prepared a wonderful garden. The garden was filled with plants and trees bearing fruit to provide food. God filled the garden with animals and birds. God filled the waters with fish. God saw that all of this creation was good. On the sixth day, God added the creation of humankind. God made these people in God's image. What did this mean? God created humans as representatives of God. God gave human beings the ability to think, to feel, and to make decisions. These people were created male and female. Spend some time this week looking at photograph albums with pictures of people who are special to your family. Say a thank you prayer for each one of them. Look with your child at pictures from when he or she was a baby. Enjoy talking about how much he or she has grown.

Creation Prayer

Thank you, God, we want to say
For making us to laugh and play.
For people living in God's way.
We thank you, God, today.
Amen.

Yummy People Cookies

Using your favorite sugar cookie recipe or commercially prepared dough, make people cookies. You can use gingerbread people cookie cutters or you can do round cookies and only make faces. Use icing, sprinkles, candy, and raisins to decorate your people. Enjoy this sweet snack. Thank God for people. Name some special friends and family.

We thank God for people.

PRESCHOOL: LESSON 10 Permission granted to photocopy for local church use. © 2003 Abingdon Press.

Preschool: Lesson 10 — **Reproducible 10B**

11 BibleZone LIVE

God's First Garden (Adam and Eve)

Enter the Zone

Bible Verse
The earth and everything on it belong to the Lord.
(Psalm 24:1)

Bible Story
Genesis 2:4-17; 3:1-13, 20-24

This Scripture is sometimes known as the second creation story. The story of Creation in Genesis 1 is an orderly story that recounts the creation of the world. It emphasizes God's power in creating the world. God spoke and it happened. God saw all that had been created and said that it was good.

In Genesis 2 and 3, the creation story focuses on the man and woman whom God has created. God forms Adam out of the ground and breathes life into him. Then God made Eve so that Adam would not be lonely. Adam and Eve are given a wonderful garden called Eden in which to live. Adam is given the task to oversee the garden, making sure that the trees and plants continue to flourish. There is only one limitation. They are not to eat from the tree in the middle of the garden: the tree of the knowledge of good and evil.

When the snake tempts Eve to eat from this tree, she knows that she should not do it. She finally gives in and offers the fruit to Adam.

The heart of the story is the disobedience to God's plan. Adam and Eve's relationship with God was forever changed because they did what they knew was wrong. Eating the fruit was choosing evil because eating the fruit separated Adam and Eve from God. Adam and Eve become afraid of God because they have done wrong. God was very disappointed with them. Yet, God clothed them and continued to love them in spite of their disobedience.

As we share this story with young children, we focus on the fact the Adam and Eve were living in the Garden of Eden. God told them to take care of the garden. There was one rule. They could not eat from one special tree, but they disobeyed. Children can relate to times of doing what Mom or Dad told them not to do.

Point out that even though God was sad that they had disobeyed, God loved Adam and Eve. Love and pray for the children that are in your class, even those who disobey.

We thank God for people.

Scope the Zone

ZONE	TIME	SUPPLIES	ZILLIES
Zoom Into the Zone			
Find the Differences	5 minutes	Reproducible 11A, markers or crayons	none
Creation Cube Game	5 minutes	Transparency 3, overhead projector, Reproducible 10B, buttons or squares of paper	none
Sneaky Snake Spirals	6 minutes	Reproducible 11B, scissors, paper punch, yarn, markers	none
BibleZone			
The Tree in the Garden	8 minutes	white paper, transparency film, stained glass paint, paintbrushes, paper punch, paint cups, water cups, scissors, fishing line, newspaper	CD
Zoo Animal Friends	5 minutes	none	zoo animal finger puppets
God's First Garden	3 minutes	socks	none
Bible Verse Buzz	5 minutes	Bible, BZ Bee	none
March a Verse	5 minutes	none	none
A Wonderful World	5 minutes	none	none
Sing a Creation Song	5 minutes	CD player	CD
LifeZone			
Happy Handprints	10 minutes	salt clay, paint, paintbrushes, rolling pin, newspapers	none
Animal Toss	3 minutes	clothesbasket	zoo animal porcupine balls
Creation Prayers	3 minutes	none	zoo animal finger puppets

Zillies® are found in the **BibleZone® LIVE FUNspirational® Kit.**

Zoom Into the Zone

Choose one or more activities to capture the attention of your children.

Supplies:
Reproducible 11A
markers or crayons

Zillies®:
none

Find the Differences

Copy the Garden of Eden picture (**Reproducible 11A**) for each child. Have the children look at the two pictures.

Ask: Can you see what is different in the two pictures? *(Give the children a chance to look at the pictures and respond.)*

Have the children color the pictures when they have found all the differences.

Say: God created Adam and Eve to live in the Garden of Eden. God told them not to eat from the tree in the middle of the garden. Today we'll hear a story about Adam and Eve.

We thank God for people.

Supplies:
Transparency 3
Reproducible 10B
buttons or squares of paper for markers

Zillies®:
none

Creation Cube Game

Make a copy of the game cube (**Transparency 3**) on poster paper. Cut out and make into a cube. This is great fun when the cube is large. Make copies of the game card (**Reproducible 10B**) for each child. Pick a child to roll the cube. When it lands, ask that child to call out the part of creation they see on the cube. All the children should then mark their card with the buttons or squares of paper. Ask another child to roll the cube. Continue until the cards are filled up. Everyone then stands up and says: "I am special. God made me."

Supplies:
Reproducible 11B
scissors
paper punch
yarn
markers or crayons

Zillies®:
none

Sneaky Snake Spirals

Copy the spiral snake (**Reproducible 11B**) for each child.

Say: There was a snake that lived in the Garden of Eden. This snake told Eve to do the wrong thing and she listened to him. We're going to make a snake spiral to remind us of the snake in the story.

Have the children color their snakes. Cut on the dark lines so that the paper begins to spiral. Punch a hole at the top. Insert a piece of yarn for hanging.

Choose one or more activities to immerse your children in the Bible story.

The Tree in the Garden

Draw a tree on half of an 8 ½ x 11 inch sheet of paper. Using a copier, copy this tree onto transparency film. (You should be able to get two pictures on each sheet of film.)

Cover the table with newspaper. Pour paint into small cups. Provide water cups for the children to rinse their brushes as they change colors.

Have the children paint the transparency with stained glass paint. This paint dries very quickly.

After the picture is dry, cut the picture in an oval shape. Punch a hole at the top of the picture. Insert a piece of fishing line for hanging.

Say: Our tree in the garden sun catchers can remind us of the story of Adam and Eve. We can remember that God loves us even when we make mistakes.

Supplies:
White paper
Transparency film,
    ½ sheet per child
stained glass paint
    (brown and green)
paintbrushes
paper punch
paint cups
water cups
scissors
fishing line
newspaper

Zillies®:
CD

Zoo Animal Friends

Say: God created people to live in the garden and take care of the rest of God's creation. These people were Adam and Eve. We have our friends, *(names of two animals)*, hopping by to visit us. We're going to play a little game with our animal friends.

Divide the children into two groups. Sit them in lines across from each other. Call one child's name. That child will hop one of the animals across to the other line. When they get to the other side, they will name something that God created. Call a child's name from the other line. They will hop their animal to the other line and name another creation. Continue until every child has had a chance.

Say: Our animal friends helped us to remember that God created a wonderful world with lots of animals, birds, fish, and us.

Supplies:
none

Zillies®:
2 animal finger
    puppets

PRESCHOOL: LESSON 11

Bible Zone Story

God's First Garden

by Beth Parr

Have the children join you in a circle. Ask the children to sign the word God *whenever they hear it in the story.*

God – Point the index finger of your right hand, with the other fingers curled down. Bring the hand down and open the palm.

Give them socks to put on their hands to be the sneaky snake and hiss when the snake appears.

God made a man named Adam to live in the beautiful Garden of Eden. This garden had all kinds of trees. Some of the trees were filled with yummy fruit. God wanted Adam to take care of the garden. Adam should make sure the trees and plants were growing.

God said, "There's one rule I need to tell you. You can eat from any tree except that one you see right in the middle of the garden." God then made a helper for Adam. This helper was a woman named Eve. Eve lived in the garden with Adam. She knew God's rule about the special tree in the middle of the garden.

One day a sneaky snake crawled up beside Eve. *(Hiss, hiss.)* The snake said, "Why don't you eat some of fruit from that tree?" Eve told the snake *(hiss, hiss)* that God did not want Adam or her to eat from that tree.

The snake *(hiss, hiss)* told Eve that it wouldn't hurt her. Finally Eve ate some of the fruit. She even gave some of the fruit to Adam. After they ate the fruit, Adam and Eve were so sad. They knew that they had done something wrong. They knew God would be disappointed.

God came to visit them in the garden. Adam and Eve hid from God because they were afraid. God knew that they had eaten from the tree.

Adam said, "Eve gave me the fruit and I ate it."

Eve said, " It was the snake's *(hiss, hiss)* fault. He tricked me and made me eat the fruit."

God was sad. He still loved Adam and Eve, but God could not let them live in the garden. Adam and Eve had to leave the beautiful Garden of Eden because they had not listened to God.

 **We thank God for people.**

In With BZ Bee

Bible Verse Buzz

Choose a child to hold the Bible open to Psalm 24:1.

Say: God made a beautiful Garden called Eden. God created a man and a woman, Adam and Eve, to live in the garden.

Say the Bible verse, "The earth and everything on it belong to the Lord" (Psalm 24:1), for the children. Have the children say the Bible verse after you.

Turn your back to the children or hide your hands underneath a table as you place the BZ Bee puppet (see page 174) on your hand. Turn around or bring the puppet out where the children can see it.

Pretend to make the puppet talk. Change your voice for the puppet:

Bzzz, Bzzz, Bzzz. Hi, everybody! I'm BZ Bee.

Bzzz, Bzzz, Bzzz. I like to taste ears. Do you have ears? Yum, yum, yum. Let me taste.

Go to each child. Encourage, but do not force each child to turn his or her ear toward BZ. Have BZ pretend to taste each child's ears. Have BZ say things like:

Mmmm. Mmmm. You taste like honey.
Bzzz. Bzzz. You taste like apples.
Yumm. Yumm. You taste like peaches.

After BZ has tasted each child's ears, **say:** Bzzz. Bzzz. Bzzz. I like to taste your ears. They're yummy. *(Rub BZ's stomach.)*

Bzzz. Bzzz. Bzzz. I like something else even more than ears. I like the Bible.

Bzzz. Bzzz. Bzzz. You heard a Bible story today about God making a special garden. What was the name of that garden? *(Eden)* Who did God make to live in the Garden of Eden? *(Adam and Eve)* Why did Adam and Eve have to leave the garden? *(because they did not obey God)*

Bzzz. Bzzz. Bzzz. God created people, just like you and me. Their names were Adam and Eve.

We thank God for people.

Bzzz. Bzzz. Bzzz. Let's say the Bible verse together: "The earth and everything on it belong to the Lord" (Psalm 24:1).

Have the children repeat the Bible verse with BZ Bee.

Have BZ Bee say good-bye to the children. Put the puppet away.

PRESCHOOL: LESSON 11

Choose one or more activities to immerse your children in the Bible story.

Supplies:
none

Zillies®:
none

March a Verse

Say the Bible verse for the children, "The earth and everything on it belong to the Lord" (Psalm 24:1).

Say: We are going to march around the room saying our Bible verse. Try to say the words with me.

March and say the Bible verse. The children will pick up the rhythm and the words.

Supplies:
none

Zillies®:
none

A Wonderful World

Use "A Wonderful World" to lead your children to the story area.

Look at me and you will see. (*Point to self, circle eyes like glasses.*)
I'm as happy, as happy can be. (*Put fingers at corners of a big smile.*)
God made the world for me and you. (*"Draw" a big circle with hands to make the world.*)
Are you happy and smiling too? (*Point away from self; put fingers at corners of smile.*)
Let's stomp, stomp, stomp.
Let's jump, jump, jump.
Let's giggle, giggle, giggle.
Let's hop, hop, hop.
Let's sit right down (*Sit in circle.*)
And now let's stop.
God made the world, everything we see. (*"Draw" a big circle with hands to make the world.*)
God made the world for you and me (*Point out and toward self.*)

Supplies:
CD player

Zillies®:
CD

Sing a Song of Creation

Say: After God created the world; God said that it was good. Let's sing a song about the people that God created. (See Lesson 10, page 124).

BibleZone® LIVE

Choose one or more activities to bring the Bible to life.

Happy Handprints

Make up a recipe of salt clay, enough for each of the children to have about a quarter of a cup.

    Salt Clay
    1 ½ cups of salt
    4 cups of flour
    1½ cups of water

Mix the salt and flour together in a mixing bowl. Slowly stir in the water. When the dough starts to stick to the spoon, knead the dough. If the dough seems too dry, add water.

Cover the table with newspapers. Give each child a ball of clay. Show them how to flatten it with the rolling pin. Have the children put their hands on the flattened clay and push down. Push hard enough to make a good indention. If you like, you can use a toothpick to write the child's name and the date on the handprint. Bake the handprints in a 300-degree oven until it has hardened. The children can then paint their handprint.

Say: God created people. People are all very different, but we are all God's creation. Our handprints are all different but God loves each one of us.

Supplies:
salt clay
paint
paintbrushes
rolling pin
newspapers

Zillies®:
none

Animal Toss

Say: We're going to play a game with our animal friends. You will have a chance to toss the animal in the basket. When you toss the animal, call out the name of one of your friends. That person will go get the animal out of the basket. We will all say our Bible verse, "The earth and everything on it belong to the Lord" (Psalm 24:1).

Enjoy playing till every child has had a turn.

Say: We can thank God for making people.

Supplies:
clothesbasket

Zillies®:
zoo animal porcupine balls

 **We thank God for people.**

Preschool: Lesson 11

Life Zone

Choose one or more activities to bring the Bible to life.

Supplies:
none

Zillies®:
zoo animal finger puppets

Creation Prayers:

Have the children sit down in a circle in the worship area.

Say: We have our friends, Monte and Tigger, with us today for our prayers.

Let one of the zoo animal finger puppets **say: Hello, boys and girls, we heard about Adam and Eve who lived in the Garden of Eden. That sure sounded like a beautiful place. God made Adam and Eve, just like God made you and me. Hey, Tigger, did you like that story?**

Let the other puppet **say: Well, I liked the story about the garden and Adam and Eve. I didn't like that snake. I didn't like when Adam and Eve disobeyed God. I'm glad God still loved them.**

Pray:
   Thank you, God, we want to say
   For making us to laugh and play.
   For people living in God's way.
   We thank you, God, today.
   Amen.

Photocopy the HomeZone newsletter to send home to the parents.

Home Zone For Parents

Bible Verse
The earth and everything on it belong to the Lord.
Psalm 24:1

Bible Story
Genesis 2:4-17; 3:1-13, 20-24

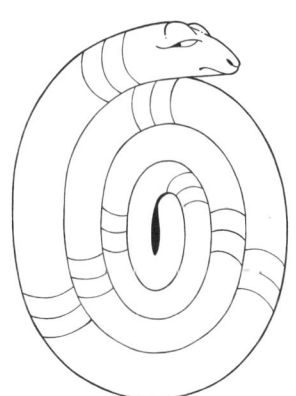

Creation Prayer

Thank you, God, we want to say
For making us to laugh and play.
For people living in God's way.
We thank you, God, today.
Amen.

Sneaky Snake Breadsticks

Using refrigerated bread stick dough, let your child make a Sneaky Snake. Use raisins for the eyes. Bake according to the directions. Enjoy eating the treat together. Remember to thank God for people. Name some special friends and family.

The heart of this story is the disobedience of Adam and Eve to God's plan. Adam and Eve's relationship with God was forever changed because they did what they knew was wrong. Eating the fruit was choosing evil because eating the fruit separated Adam and Eve from God. Adam and Eve become afraid of God because they had done wrong. God was very disappointed with them. Yet, God clothed them and continued to love them in spite of their disobedience.

As we talk with young children about this story, we talk about God creating Adam and Eve. We know Adam and Eve were wrong to disobey God. The children can relate to the fact that Adam and Eve did what was wrong, even though God told them not to. They've made that mistake with you.

God loved Adam and Eve, though God was very unhappy that they had done the wrong thing. This can be one of our guiding examples as parents, loving our child while being unhappy over the action. Your child can probably relate to Adam and Eve's feelings of guilt when God found out they had done the wrong thing. Loving our children even when they do what is wrong is following the example of God.

We thank God for people.

Reproducible 11A

Permission granted to photocopy for local church use. © 2003 Abingdon Press.

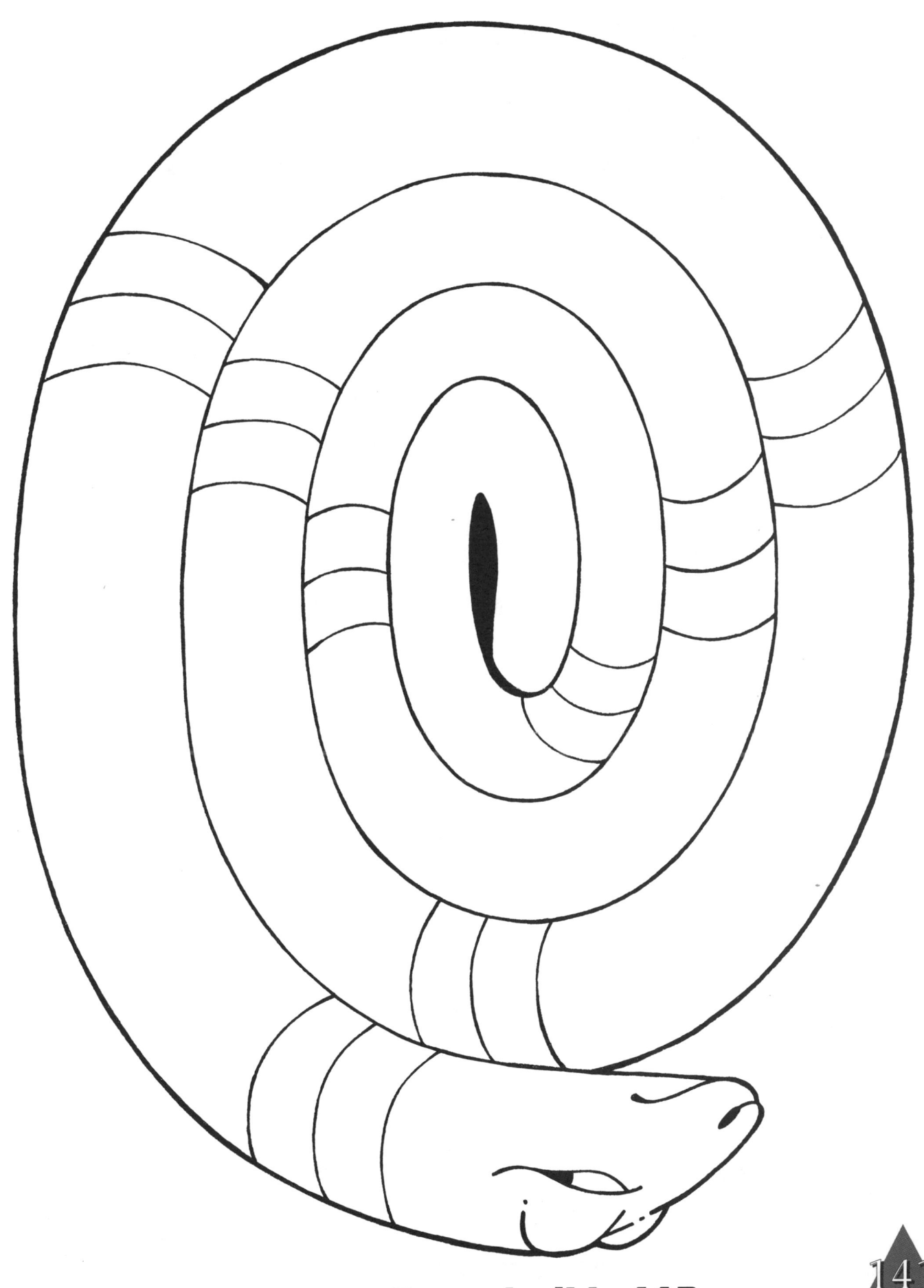

PRESCHOOL: LESSON 11

Reproducible 11B

Permission granted to photocopy for local church use. © 2003 Abingdon Press.

12 Bible LIVE

The Naming

Enter the Zone

Bible Verse
The earth and everything on it belong to the Lord.
(Psalm 24:1)

Bible Story
Genesis 2:18-24

After God had created the man and placed him in the Garden of Eden, God made animals and birds.

God knew it was not good for man to be lonely, living all alone. God brought the animals and the birds to the man to see what names he would give to them. The man gave names to the tame animals, to the birds, and to the wild animals. Through this act, God gave people power over the other animals of the earth.

God gave Adam responsibility for the garden. Adam was to take care of all of God's creation. He was to make sure that the plants and trees were growing. It was important to make sure that all the animals had enough to eat. This was God's creation and Adam was to help care for it.

After God brought the animals to Adam to be named, God saw that the animals were not the right kind of helper for the man. God then created Eve. Adam immediately knew that she was like him. Adam called her "woman" because she came from him.

Later Adam named this woman Eve. Eve in Hebrew is very close to the word for living. By naming his companion Eve, Adam was affirming that she was to be blessed with children. Adam's name in Hebrew is the word for man. This comes from the same word as *soil*, because man was made from the soil.

Naming was an important ritual in Bible times. Names conveyed hopes and dreams. Names conveyed changes in one's life. When God gave Adam the opportunity to name all the other living things, God was giving Adam great power.

Young children love to hear and see their names. They will enjoy the story of Adam naming the animals and the birds. As you talk about the names of Adam and Eve and the other living creatures, invite them to talk about their names.

God plans for people to take care of the world.

Scope the Zone

ZONE	TIME	SUPPLIES	ZILLIES
Zoom Into the Zone			
The Naming Game	10 minutes	Reproducible 12A, instant camera and film, construction paper, markers, scissors, brads, paper punch, glue	none
Creation Cube Game	5 minutes	Transparency 3, overhead projector, buttons or paper, Reproducible 10B	none
BibleZone			
What Is My Name?	5 minutes	Reproducible 12B, glue, construction paper, scissors, paper punch, yarn	none
Zoo Animal Friends	5 minutes	none	zoo animal finger puppets
The Naming	5 minutes	none	none
Bible Verse Buzz	3 minutes	Bible, BZ Bee	none
March a Verse	5 minutes	none	none
A Wonderful World	3 minutes	none	none
Sing a Creation Song	3 minutes	CD player	CD
LifeZone			
Special Names	5 minutes	poster paper, alphabet letters, decorations, glue	none
Animal Toss	3 minutes	clothesbasket	zoo animal porcupine balls
Creation Prayers	2 minutes	none	inflatable elephant and rings

Zillies® are found in the **BibleZone® LIVE FUNspirational® Kit**.

PRESCHOOL: LESSON 12

Zoom Into the Zone

Choose one or more activities to capture the attention of your children.

Supplies:
Reproducible 12A
construction paper (cut in 4 ½ x 6 inch pieces)
instant camera and film
markers or crayons
scissors
brads
paper punch
glue

Zillies®:
none

The Naming Game

Copy the naming pictures (**Reproducible 12A**) for each child. Color the pictures with crayons or markers. Have the children cut the pictures apart. Glue the pictures on pieces of construction paper. Take a picture of each child. Have the child glue his or her picture on the last piece of construction paper. To make the name book, put the pages together and punch two holes in the side. Insert the brads to hold the pages together.

Say: God brought the animals to Adam so that Adam could give them names. Let's see if we know the names of these animals and birds. *(Ask the children to look at each page and name the animal.)* **On the last page is a picture of someone very special. God loves you.**

Supplies:
Transparency 3
overhead projector
Reproducible 10B
buttons or squares of paper for markers

Zillies®:
none

Creation Cube Game

Make a copy of the game cube (**Transparency 3**) on poster paper. Cut out and make into a cube. This is great fun when the cube is large. Make copies of the game card (**Reproducible 10B**) for each child. Pick a child to roll the cube. When it lands, ask that child to call out the part of creation they see on the cube. All the children should then mark their card with the buttons or squares of paper. Ask another child to roll the cube. Continue until the cards are filled up. Everyone then stands up and says: "I am special. God made me."

God plans for people to take care of the world.

BibleZone® LIVE

Choose one or more activities to immerse your children in the Bible story.

What Is My Name?

Copy enough of the animal pictures **(Reproducible 12B)** so that each child will have a nametag. Cut the animal pictures apart and give one to each child. To make the nametag, have the children glue their picture on the construction paper strip. Punch holes in each corner of the construction paper. Thread the yarn through the holes and tie it in a knot. Choose one child to be Adam. Other children will put their nametag around their neck.

Say: Look at your nametag. Do you know what kind of animal you are? *(Help the children who don't know what animal they are.)* **Think about what sound your animal makes.**

Have "Adam" sit in a chair. Bring the animals to him one at a time or in groups if you have more than one of an animal. The children will make the sound of their animals. Adam will then give them a name. You can play this several times, changing Adams if the children are enjoying it.

Say: God wanted Adam to take care of the garden and all the animals in it. God asked Adam to give names to the animals.

Supplies:
Reproducible 12B
strips of construction paper
scissors
glue
paper punch
yarn

Zillies®:
none

Zoo Animal Friends

Say: God created people to live in the garden and take care of the rest of God's creation. These people were Adam and Eve. We have our friends, *(names of animals)*, **hopping by to visit us. We're going to play a little game with our animal friends.**

Divide the children into two groups. Sit them in lines across from each other. Call one child's name. That child will hop one of the animals across to the other line. When they get to the other side, they will name something that God created. Call a child's name from the other line. They will hop their animal to the other line and name another creation. Continue until every child has had a chance.

Say: Our animal friends helped us to remember that God created a wonderful world with lots of animals, birds, fish, and us. God asked Adam to give names to all of God's creation.

Supplies:
none

Zillies®:
2 animal finger puppets

PRESCHOOL: LESSON 12

Bible  Story

The Naming

by Beth Parr

Have the children join you in a circle.
Teach the children "Do You Know?" to the tune of "Do You Know the Muffin Man?" Have them sing it during the story:
  Do you know what my name is?
  What my name is? What my name is?
  Do you know what my name is?
  Tell me if you can.
  (Then ask the children to guess the name.)

God made Adam and placed him in the Garden of Eden. God didn't want Adam to be lonely so he created animals. God created tame animals and wild animals. God created birds. There were so many creatures in the garden now.

God said to Adam, "I want you to take care of this world I have created. I want you to give names to all of the animals." One by one God brought the animals to Adam to receive their names.

There was an animal that loved to climb in trees. He could swing from branch to branch. He could hang by his tail.

Do you know what my name is? What my name is, what my name is? Do you know what my name is? Tell me if you can.
(Ask the children to guess the name: monkey.)

There was an animal that walked very slowly. Its tail switched from side to side. This animal could give milk to people to drink.
(Have the children sing "Do You Know?" Then ask them to guess the name: cow.)

There was a bird that could fly very high. It had a sharp beak and claws. This bird could spread its wings very wide.

(Have the children sing "Do You Know?" Then ask them to guess the name: eagle.)

There was an animal with a very long neck. This animal loved to eat the leaves way up in the top of the trees. This animal also had spots.
(Have the children sing "Do You Know?" Then ask them to guess the name: giraffe.)

There was an animal that was round and fat. He loved to roll and play in the mud. He had a short curly tail.
(Have the children sing "Do You Know?" Then ask them to guess the name: pig.)

There was an animal that had lots of hair around his neck. He could roar very loudly. He thought he was king of the jungle.
(Have the children sing "Do You Know?" Then ask them to guess the name: lion.)

God saw that these animals weren't the right kind of helpers for Adam. God made a helper for Adam. When Adam saw her, he knew that she was like him. He knew they could work together.
(Have the children sing "Do You Know?" Then ask them to guess who this is: Eve.)

God created the world and gave each person the responsibility for helping to take care of it.

In With BZ Bee

Bible Verse Buzz

Choose a child to hold the Bible open to Psalm 24:1.

Say: God made a beautiful Garden called Eden. God created a man and a woman, Adam and Eve to live in the garden. God wanted Adam and Eve to take care of the garden.

Say the Bible verse, "The earth and everything on it belong to the Lord" (Psalm 24:1), for the children. Have the children say the Bible verse after you.

Turn your back to the children or hide your hands underneath a table as you place the BZ Bee puppet (see page 174) on your hand. Turn around or bring the puppet out where the children can see it.

Pretend to make the puppet talk. Change your voice for the puppet:

Bzzz, Bzzz, Bzzz. Hi, everybody! I'm BZ Bee.

Bzzz, Bzzz, Bzzz. I like to taste ears. Do you have ears? Yum, yum, yum. Let me taste.

Go to each child. Encourage, but do not force each child to turn his or her ear toward BZ. Have BZ pretend to taste each child's ears. Have BZ say things like:

Mmmm. Mmmm. You taste like honey.
Bzzz. Bzzz. You taste like apples.
Yumm. Yumm. You taste like peaches.

After BZ has tasted each child's ears, **say:**
Bzzz. Bzzz. Bzzz. I like to taste your ears. They're yummy. *(Rub BZ's stomach.)*

Bzzz. Bzzz. Bzzz. I like something else even more than ears. I like the Bible.

Bzzz. Bzzz. Bzzz. You heard a Bible story today about God making a special garden. What was the man's name that God placed in the garden? *(Adam)* **What was the name of the woman God created to help him?** *(Eve)* **Why did God bring the animals to Adam?** *(so that he could give them names)*

Bzzz. Bzzz. Bzzz. God created people, just like you and me. Their names were Adam and Eve. God wanted them to take care of the world. God wants us to help care for the world too.

God plans for people to take care of the world.

Bzzz. Bzzz. Bzzz. Let's say the Bible verse together: "The earth and everything on it belong to the Lord" (Psalm 24:1).

Have the children repeat the Bible verse with BZ Bee.

Have BZ Bee say good-bye to the children. Put the puppet away.

Choose one or more activities to immerse your children in the Bible story.

Supplies:
none

Zillies®:
none

March a Verse

Say the Bible verse for the children, "The earth and everything on it belong to the Lord" (Psalm 24:1).

Say: We are going to march around the room saying our Bible verse. Try to say the words with me.

March and say the Bible verse. The children will pick up the rhythm and the words.

Supplies:
none

Zillies®:
none

A Wonderful World

Use "A Wonderful World" to lead your children to the story area.

Look at me and you will see. (*Point to self, circle eyes like glasses.*)
I'm as happy, as happy can be. (*Put fingers at corners of a big smile.*)
God made the world for me and you. ("*Draw*" *a big circle with hands to make the world.*)
Are you happy and smiling too? (*Point away from self; put fingers at corners of smile.*)
Let's stomp, stomp, stomp.
Let's jump, jump, jump.
Let's giggle, giggle, giggle.
Let's hop, hop, hop.
Let's sit right down (*Sit in circle.*)
And now let's stop.
God made the world, everything we see. ("*Draw*" *a big circle with hands to make the world.*)
God made the world for you and me (*Point out and toward self.*)

Supplies:
CD player

Zillies®:
CD

Sing a Creation Song

Say: After God created the world; God said that it was good. Let's sing a song about the people that God created. (See Lesson 10, page 124.)

BibleZone® LIVE

Choose one or more activities to bring the Bible to life.

Special Names

Fold each piece of poster paper in half lengthwise to make a tent card. Have the children find the letters that go in their name. Younger children may need some help with this activity. Glue the letters on the tent cards. The children can do both sides, if you want. Let the children decorate the cards with any of the materials you have provided.

Say: **Our parents gave us special names, just like Adam gave names to the animals. We can remember that God loves us and knows us by name. We can help take care of the earth.**

Animal Toss

Say: **We're going to play a game with our animal friends. You will have a chance to toss the animal in the basket. When you toss the animal, call out the name of one of your friends. That person will go get the animal out of the basket. We will all say our Bible verse, "The earth and everything on it belong to the Lord" (Psalm 24:1).**

Enjoy playing till every child has had a turn.

Say: **We can thank God for making people.**

 **God plans for people to take care of the world.**

Supplies:
poster paper (12 inches long by 8 inches wide), 1 per child
bubble alphabet letters
ribbons, foam pieces, paper scraps, glue

Zillies®:
none

Supplies:
clothesbasket

Zillies®:
none

PRESCHOOL: LESSON 12

Life

Choose one or more activities to bring the Bible to life.

Supplies:
none

Zillies®:
inflatable elephant and rings

Creation Prayers:

Have the children sit down in a circle in the worship area. Place Ellie the Elephant in the middle of the circle.

Say: Today we have Ellie the Elephant back to visit with us. She's going to help us play a little game. Let's sit in a circle. When I call your name, I want you to pick up one of the rings and put it on Ellie's trunk.

Then, we'll all say our Bible verse. "The earth and everything in it belong to the Lord" (Psalm 24:1).

Pray:
   Thank you, God, we want to say
   For making us to laugh and play.
   For people living in God's way.
   We thank you, God, today.
   Amen.

Photocopy the HomeZone newsletter to send home to the parents.

 **God plans for people to take care of the world.**

Home Zone For Parents

Bible Verse
The earth and everything on it belong to the Lord.
Psalm 24:1

Bible Story
Genesis 2:18-24

In our story today, God creates Adam and places him in the Garden of Eden. God plans for Adam to take care of the garden. God does not want Adam to be lonely, so God creates animals of many kinds and birds to fly in the air. God asks Adam to name the animals. Adam gives a name to each living creature.

God sees that these creatures are not the right kind of helper for Adam. God creates a woman to be Adam's helper. Adam sees that she is like him. He names her Eve. Together they work to take care of the garden.

We talked today about God's plan for people to take care of the world. Talk with your child about ways that you can help take care of the world.

Adam gave names to all the animals. Enjoy looking at your child's naming book, baby book or photographs of your child. Talk with your child about his or her name.

Recycling Opportunities

Involve your child in helping to take care of the world. You could gather up newspapers or aluminum cans for recycling. You could clean up trash around your home. *(Be careful of the kinds of trash your child may find.)* Take plastic bags back to the grocery store to be reused.

Name Cakes

Using metal letter cookie cutters, make name pancakes. Pour pancake batter into cookie cutters. Remove the cookie cutter when the batter sets. Be careful. The cookie cutters can get quite hot. Enjoy eating your names with butter and syrup.

Creation Prayer

Thank you, God, we want to say
For making us to laugh and play.
For people living in God's way.
We thank you, God, today.
Amen.

God plans for people to take care of the world.

PRESCHOOL: LESSON 12   Permission granted to photocopy for local church use. © 2003 Abingdon Press.

Reproducible 12A

Permission granted to photocopy for local church use. © 2003 Abingdon Press.

Bird

Beaver

Rabbit

Dog

Bear

Mouse

PRESCHOOL: LESSON 12 **Reproducible 12B**
Permission granted to photocopy for local church use. © 2003 Abingdon Press.

13

A Time For All Things

Enter the Zone

Bible Verse
Everything on earth has its own time and its own season.

(Ecclesiastes 3:1)

Bible Story
Ecclesiastes 3:1-15

This familiar passage from the book of Ecclesiastes reminds us that God is in control of all that is. Everything that happens in our world happens according to God's time. While we cannot always understand why some things happen when they do, we can seek comfort in knowing that God is always with us.

This passage speaks not just of the passage of seasons of the years, but likewise speaks of seasons of life. This consistency of life can provide security to us.

The author of this passage concludes that understanding all of God's timing is beyond our ability. It is far better to relax and enjoy the life that God has given us. It is reassuring to know that God is in control. This passage can be very abstract for young children. Looking at the seasons of the year can provide a way for children to look at our changing world. We can talk of the seasons as part of God's plan for the world. While every season is not exactly the same, there is similarity to the progress of the year. One of the challenges in talking about seasons is that seasons are different across our nation. Be aware of the seasons in your area and adapt the activities as needed. Snow may never be seen in your part of the country. You may want to talk about winter as rainy instead. You could also introduce the idea of how seasons are different in different parts of our world.

In a world where there is so much that we can't count on, it brings comfort to know that God has planned for our world and for our lives. We can thank God for the seasons that remind us of the wonder of God's creation.

We thank God for the seasons.

Scope the Zone

ZONE	TIME	SUPPLIES	ZILLIES
Zoom Into the Zone			
Trees of the Season Crowns	10 minutes	Reproducible 13A, paper confetti, construction paper, construction paper strip, markers or crayons, scissors, glue, stapler	none
Season Shake	5 minutes	crowns made earlier	none
BibleZone			
Time for Everything	8 minutes	Reproducible 13B, 9-inch-paper plates, markers or crayons, scissors, glue, brads	none
Zoo Animal Friends	5 minutes	none	2 animal finger puppets
A Time for All Things	8 minutes	none	none
Bible Verse Buzz	5 minutes	Bible, BZ Bee	none
Hop a Verse	5 minutes	none	none
A Wonderful World	5 minutes	none	none
Sing a Song of Praise	5 minutes	CD player	CD
LifeZone			
Weather Relay	10 minutes	clothing for different kinds of weather, clothesbasket	none
Winter Soap Painting	6 minutes	see p. 161	none
Colors of the Season	6 minutes	see p. 161	zoo animal porcupine balls
Creation Prayers	5 minutes	none	inflatable elephant and rings

Zillies® are found in the **BibleZone® LIVE FUNspirational® Kit.**

PRESCHOOL: LESSON 13

Zoom Into the Zone

Choose one or more activities to capture the attention of your children.

Supplies:
Reproducible 13A (1 copy per child)
paper confetti (punched out holes of red, orange, green, and yellow construction paper.)
construction paper strip
markers or crayons
scissors
glue
stapler

Zillies®:
none

Trees of the Season Crowns

Copy the seasonal tree page (**Reproducible 13A**) for each child. Have the children color the pictures of the trees. They can glue the construction paper confetti to the trees to make autumn leaves and spring and summer leaves. Cut out the trees. Young children may need help with cutting. To create a crown, size each construction paper strip to fit each child's head. Have the children glue their trees to the crown. Staple the crown together to fit.

Say: Our tree crowns remind us of the different seasons of the year. The weather is different at different times of the year. The trees look different. God planned for the different seasons of the year.

We thank God for the seasons.

Supplies:
crowns made above

Zillies®:
none

Season Shake

Have the children put on their crowns. Form a circle. Use poem to talk about seasons. Ask the children to shake their bodies when you say the words *shake, shake, shake*.

We'll shake, shake, shake
And then we'll stop.
What season is it when it's hot? (*summer*)
We'll shake, shake, shake
And then we'll stop.
What season is it when the leaves turn colors? (*fall*)
We'll shake, shake, shake
And then we'll stop.
What season is it when the flowers begin to grow? (*spring*)
We'll shake, shake, shake
And then we'll stop.
What season is it when it's cold? (*winter*)
We'll shake, shake, shake
And then we'll stop.
We'll thank God and hop, hop, hop.

BibleZone® LIVE

Choose one or more activities to immerse your children in the Bible story.

Time for Everything

Copy a clock **(Reproducible 13B)** for each child. Cut out the clock face, the arrows, and the small pictures of things we do during the day and during the year. Have the children glue the clock face on the paper plate. Help the children to punch a hole in the center of the plate and at the ends of the arrows. Put a brad through the holes to make the hands of the clock. Have the children color the small pictures. Glue these onto the face of the clock.

Say: God planned that there would be a time for everything. God made the seasons of the year. God planned for the leaves to fall from the tree. God planned for rain and snow to fall. God planned for us to enjoy all that we do during the day.

Zoo Animal Friends

Say: God planned for different seasons in the year. God planned for winter, for spring, for summer, and for fall. We have our friends, *(name of animals)*, **hopping by to visit us. We're going to play a little game with our animal friends.**

Divide the children into two groups. Sit them in lines across from each other. Call one child's name. That child will hop one of the animals across to the other line. When they get to the other side, they will name their favorite time of the year. Call a child's name from the other line. They will hop their animal to the other line and name their favorite time of the year. Continue until every child has had a chance.

Say: Our friends *(name the animals)* **helped us to remember that God created a wonderful world with time for different seasons and activities.**

Supplies:
Reproducible 13B
9-inch paper plates
markers or crayons
scissors
glue
brads

Zillies®:
none

Supplies:
none

Zillies®:
2 animal finger puppets

PRESCHOOL: LESSON 13

Bible  Story

A Time for All Things
by Beth Parr

Have the children join you in a circle.

Give the children crepe paper streamers *(orange, white, green, and yellow)*.

Say: We are going to use our streamers to remind us of the seasons of the year. When we talk about fall, we'll wave our orange streamer. When we talk about winter, we'll wave our white streamer. When we talk about spring, we'll wave our green streamer. When we talk about summer, we'll wave our yellow streamer.

God planned this world very carefully. God made day and night. God made oceans and dry land. God made plants that everyone could eat. God made the sky with the sun, moon and stars. God made trees, animals, birds, fish and people. God planned for there to be different seasons of the year. In the fall *(wave orange streamer)*, it's a little cool. The leaves are changing colors. Pumpkins are growing in the pumpkin patch. Fall is a time to rake leaves. It is a time to wear a sweater and long pants. We celebrate Thanksgiving in the fall. *(Wave orange streamer.)*

The season of winter *(wave white streamer)* can be very cold. We have white streamers because some people have snow in the winter. Some places have ice on the ponds. Some places only have rain. In the winter, we wear more clothes to stay warm. The trees often don't have leaves, unless they are always green like Christmas trees. We celebrate Christmas in the winter. *(Wave white streamer.)*

God planned for the season of spring. *(Wave green streamer.)* It's beginning to get warmer. The flowers are starting to bloom. The trees are growing new green leaves. Sometimes spring also means rain. The rain waters the ground and helps all the plants to grow. We celebrate Easter in the spring. *(Wave green streamer.)*

There's one other season God planned for this world. That is the season of summer. *(Wave yellow streamer.)* We wave a yellow streamer because the sun is bright and warm. We like to be outside in the summer. People enjoy swimming in the summer. The leaves on the trees are still green. It's often very hot. We wear shorts and sandals to stay cool. We celebrate Pentecost in the summer. *(Wave yellow streamer.)*

God planned for the seasons of the year. We can thank God for the beauty of each season. Let's wave all our streamers to say thank you to God.

 **We thank God for the seasons.**

BibleZone® LIVE

In With BZ Bee

Bible Verse Buzz

Choose a child to hold the Bible open to Ecclesiastes 3:1.

Say: God planned for different seasons of year. Some seasons are hot and others are cold. We can enjoy the world God made for us at all times of the year.

Say the Bible verse, "Everything on earth has its own time and its own season" (Ecclesiastes 3:1) for the children. Have the children say the Bible verse after you.

Turn your back to the children or hide your hands underneath a table as you place the BZ Bee puppet (see page 174) on your hand. Turn around or bring the puppet out where the children can see it.

Pretend to make the puppet talk. Change your voice for the puppet:

Bzzz, Bzzz, Bzzz. Hi, everybody! I'm BZ Bee.

Bzzz, Bzzz, Bzzz. I like to taste ears. Do you have ears? Yum, yum, yum. Let me taste.

Go to each child. Encourage, but do not force each child to turn his or her ear toward BZ. Have BZ pretend to taste each child's ears. Have BZ say things like:

Mmmm. Mmmm. You taste like honey.
Bzzz. Bzzz. You taste like apples.
Yumm. Yumm. You taste like peaches.

After BZ has tasted each child's ears, **say:**
Bzzz. Bzzz. Bzzz. I like to taste your ears. They're yummy. *(Rub BZ's stomach.)* **Bzzz. Bzzz. Bzzz. I like something else even more than ears. I like the Bible.**

Bzzz. Bzzz. Bzzz. You heard a story today about God planning for special times during the year. What are the seasons of the year? *(fall, winter, spring, summer)* **Who planned for the seasons of the year?** *(God)*

Bzzz. Bzzz. Bzzz. God created our world. God planned for there to be different seasons of the year. God planned that everything would have a time.

We thank God for the seasons.

Bzzz. Bzzz. Bzzz. Let's say the Bible verse together: "Everything on earth has its own time and its own season" (Ecclesiastes 3:1).

Have the children repeat the Bible verse with BZ Bee.

Have BZ Bee say good-bye to the children. Put the puppet away.

Bible

Choose one or more activities to immerse your children in the Bible story.

Supplies:
none

Zillies®:
none

Hop a Verse

Say the Bible verse for the children, "Everything on earth has its own time and its own season" (Ecclesiastes 3:1).

Say: We are going to hop around the room saying our Bible verse. Try to say the words with me.

Hop and say the Bible verse. The children will pick up the rhythm and the words.

Supplies:
none

Zillies®:
none

A Wonderful World

Use "A Wonderful World" to lead your children to the story area.

Look at me and you will see. (*Point to self, circle eyes like glasses.*)
I'm as happy, as happy can be. (*Put fingers at corners of a big smile.*)
God made the world for me and you. ("*Draw" a big circle with hands to make the world.*)
Are you happy and smiling too? (*Point away from self; put fingers at corners of smile.*)
Let's stomp, stomp, stomp.
Let's jump, jump, jump.
Let's giggle, giggle, giggle.
Let's hop, hop, hop.
Let's sit right down (*Sit in circle.*)
And now let's stop.
God made the world, everything we see. ("*Draw" a big circle with hands to make the world.*)
God made the world for you and me (*Point out and toward self.*)

Supplies:
CD player

Zillies®:
CD

Sing a Song of Praise

Say: God created the seasons of the year for us to enjoy. Let's sing a song about praising.

Sing "Praisin'" with the **CD (Track 13)** and do the motions. (See Lesson 1, page 16.)

© 1996 Cokesbury

BibleZone® LIVE

Choose one or more activities to bring the Bible to life.

Weather Relay

Ask the children to line up on one side of the room. Place the basket full of clothes on the other side of the room. Call a child's name. Tell them what the weather is like. They should run to the basket and find the right kind of clothes to wear. Hold the clothes up for others to see. Everyone will say: Thank you, God, for _____ (the weather). Continue to play until all the children who would like have had a chance to pick the clothes.

Say: God planned for different season so that we could enjoy doing different things throughout the year. We can thank God for the seasons.

Supplies:
clothing for different kinds of weather: raincoat, sweater, shorts, bathing suit, mittens, toboggan, and so forth
clothesbasket

Zillies®:
none

Seasonal Painting

Option 1: Place a cup of detergent in the bowl. Pour in one half cup of warm water. Let the children take turns using the whisk or eggbeater to beat the mixture until it becomes fluffy. Use a spoon to place a small amount of the mixture on each child's paper. Have the children use the toothbrushes to paint a snowy picture.

Say: We can thank God for winter and for snow. We can thank God for seasons.

Option 2: Cover the work area with recycled newspaper. Spoon small amounts of green, yellow, orange, red tempera paint onto pieces of drawing paper.

Say: We're going to paint a picture of the seasons with our zoo animal porcupine balls. Think about all the colors of the seasons. Paint swirls to create pictures of the colors of the seasons.

Supplies:
mild detergent flakes
warm water
whisk or hand egg-beater
large bowl
dark-colored construction paper
toothbrushes
tempera paint (yellow, red, orange, green)
drawing paper
newspaper
spoon

Zillies®:
zoo animal porcupine balls

 **We thank God for the seasons.**

PRESCHOOL: LESSON 13

Life

Choose one or more activities to bring the Bible to life.

Supplies:
none

Zillies®:
inflatable elephant and rings

Creation Prayers

Have the children sit down in a circle in the worship area. Place Ellie the Elephant in the middle of the circle.

Say: Today we have Ellie the Elephant back to visit with us. She's going to help us play a game. When I call your name, I want you to pick up one of the rings and put it on Ellie's trunk. Then, we'll all say our Bible verse. "Everything on earth has its own time and its own season" (Ecclesiastes 3:1).

Pray:
Thank you, God, we want to say
For making fall and winter days.
For spring and summer when we play.
We thank you, God, today.
Amen.

Photocopy the HomeZone newsletter to send home to the parents.

Home Zone For Parents

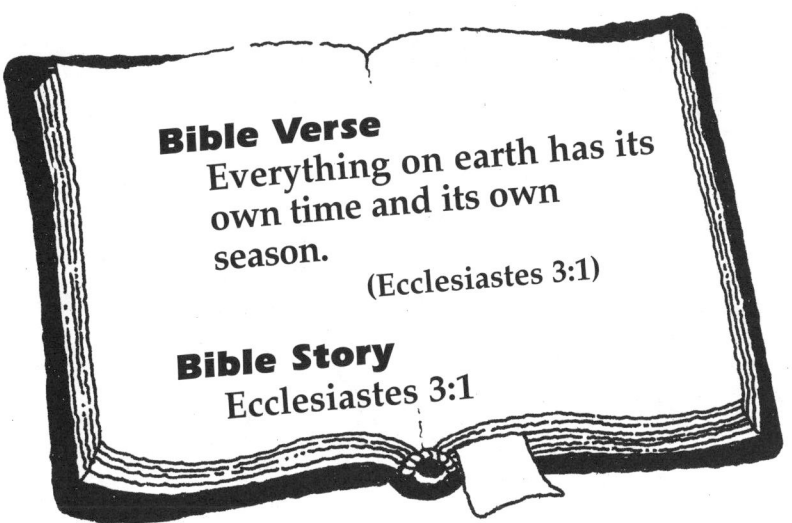

Bible Verse
Everything on earth has its own time and its own season.
(Ecclesiastes 3:1)

Bible Story
Ecclesiastes 3:1

Our Bible story today helped us to think about God's plan for the seasons. As we enjoy the seasons of the year, we can know that God is in control. God has planned for there to be a time for everything.

In a world where there is so much that we can't count on, it brings comfort to know that God has planned for our world and for our lives. We can thank God for the seasons that remind us of the wonder of God's creation. Play a game with your child about the weather and the seasons of the year. Ask them what they would wear on a particular day (rainy, winter, summer, and so on).

Look at the trees where you live. Can you tell what season it is by the leaves?

Creation Prayer

Thank you, God, we want to say
For making fall and winter days.
For spring and summer when we play.
We thank you, God, today.
Amen.

Sing a Song of Seasons

Enjoy singing with your child to the tune of "Do You Know the Muffin Man?"
    For everything there is a season,
    Is a season, is a season.
    For everything there is a season;
    God made them all.

We thank God for the seasons.

PRESCHOOL: LESSON 13   Permission granted to photocopy for local church use. © 2003 Abingdon Press.

Reproducible 13A

Permission granted to photocopy for local church use. © 2003 Abingdon Press.

Preschool: Lesson 13 **Reproducible 13B**

Game Zone

Walk This Way

Call the children by name either one at a time or in groups of two or three. Instruct the children to move to the designated place with one of the following suggestions.

Pretend you are a fish swimming in a river.
Pretend you are a bird flying in the sky.
Pretend you are a crab walking on the sand.
Pretend you are an elephant walking on the plain.
Pretend you are a bumblebee flying from flower to flower.

True or False Game

Make the following statements about God's world. If the statement is true, have the children nod their heads yes and say, "Yes! God's world is good!" If the statement if false, have the children shake their heads no and say, "No! Not in God's world!"

God made clouds to float up in the sky.
(Yes! God's world is good!)
God made great big whales to swim in the sea.
(Yes! God's world is good!)
God made cats to bark, "Woof, woof, woof!"
(Not! Not in God's world!)
God made dogs to bark, "Woof, woof, woof!"
(Yes! God's world is good!)
God made elephants to fly in the sky.
(No! Not in God's world!)

Snack Zone

Roundabout Rice Cake

You will need: one rice cake for each child, cream cheese, and a variety of pre-sliced vegetables or fruits for the children to use as decorations.

Let the children be creative and decorate the top of their rice cakes with the presliced vegetables. Talk about what it must have been like to be God and create all the universe.

Banana Tree Treats

You will need: lettuce leaf, pineapple rings, bananas, sliced fruits such as grapes, cut up pears, cherries, cut up peaches, strawberries or other berries, apple slices or chunks, and cheese cut into cubes.

Place a lettuce leaf on the salad plate. Place a pineapple ring on the lettuce leaf. Peel the banana and cut it in half. Stand the cut end of the banana half in the center of the pineapple to resemble a tree trunk. Place a toothpick through a selected piece of fruit. Stick the other end of the toothpick into the top area of the banana. Each toothpick with a piece of fruit will represent a branch on the banana tree.

Art Zone

Plastic Bag Art

You will need: recycled newspaper, plaster of Paris, a spoon, resealable plastic sandwich bags, tablespoon, powdered tempera paint, water

1. Scoop plaster of Paris into a resealable sandwich bag.
2. Add 1 tablespoon powdered tempera paint to the plaster.
3. Pour in enough water to form a soft dough.
4. Squeeze the plastic bag to mix the water, paint, and plaster.
5. As the plaster hardens, mold the bag into an animal shape.
6. When the sculpture is hard, remove it from the bag.
7. Glue the sculpture to a wooden base.
8. Let the child tell you about his or her animal—where it lives, what it eats, and so forth.

Make a Garden

You will need: play dough, a heavy paper plate, seeds and weeds (dry flowers, leaves, nuts, pinecones, rocks, seed pods, thistles, twigs, shells)

1. Place a ball of playdough in the center of a heavy paper plate.
2. Spread the playdough out until it covers the bottom of the playdough. Add as much playdough as is necessary to cover the plate.
3. Press the natural items into the playdough to make a "garden."
4. Place the finished garden where everyone can admire it.

Remember in preschool art: It is the process not the product that is important.

PRESCHOOL **Reproducible 7C**
Permission granted to photocopy for local church use. © 2003 Abingdon Press.

BibleZone LIVE	BibleZone LIVE
BibleZone LIVE	BibleZone LIVE
BibleZone LIVE	BibleZone LIVE
BibleZone LIVE	BibleZone LIVE

All About

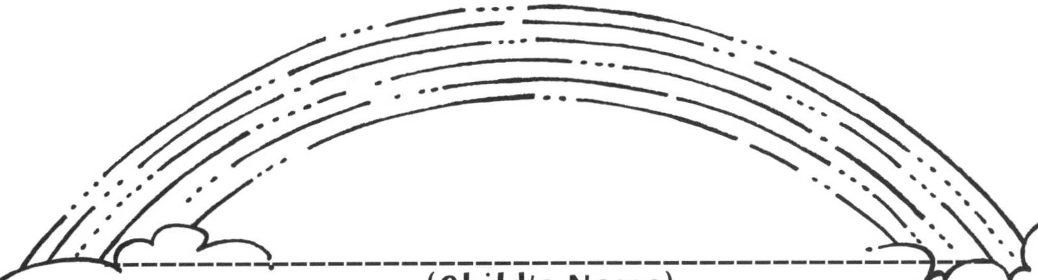

_____
(Child's Name)

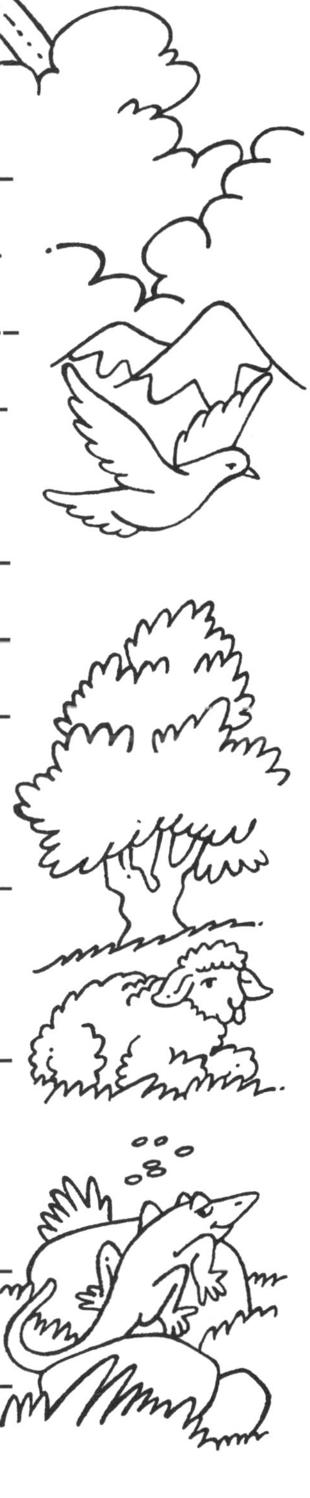

Parent's Name _____

Address _____

_____ Telephone No. _____

Child's Birthday _____ Age _____

Child's Brothers and Sisters:

Name _____ Age _____

Name _____ Age _____

Name _____ Age _____

Grandparents or other relatives your child sees often and is close to:

_____

Nursery school, daycare, or other programs your child attends:

_____

Allergies or situations in your child's life that the teacher should know:

_____

Parents will be at

_____

Permission granted to photocopy for local church use. © 2003 Abingdon Press.

Preschool — **Reproducible 9C** — 173
Permission granted to photocopy for local church use. © 2003 Abingdon Press.